Edward Augustus Warriner

The Gate Called Beautiful

An Institute of Christian Socilogy

Edward Augustus Warriner

The Gate Called Beautiful
An Institute of Christian Socilogy

ISBN/EAN: 9783337165765

Printed in Europe, USA, Canada, Australia, Japan

Cover: Foto ©Lupo / pixelio.de

More available books at **www.hansebooks.com**

THE
GATE CALLED BEAUTIFUL

An Institute of Christian Sociology

BY

EDWARD A. WARRINER

Author of "Kear," "I Am That I Am," Etc.

*"And the multitude of them that believed were of one heart
and one soul; neither said any of them that aught of the things
he possessed was his own, but they had all things common."—
Acts iv: 32.*

NEW YORK

THOMAS WHITTAKER

2 AND 3 BIBLE HOUSE

1898

CONTENTS

3

4 CONTENTS

BOOK FOURTH
APPLIED CHRISTIANITY

SPECULATIVE PROLOGUE.

SUBSTANCE, NATURE, AND ART.

SPECULATIVE philosophy, whereby the true
and ultimate principles and possibilities of our
being may be accurately defined, and when
practically applied may be realized in the outward and visible conditions of our social life—
although in times past held in very high esteem
—has in the present generation fallen into disrepute. This depreciation has been brought
about in part by limiting its use to the development of what is called natural science, the
truths of whose theories may be, and to a great
extent have been, positively demonstrated and
utilized by experiment, but chiefly by great increase in material riches, whereby naturally,
and in a measure necessarily, most men have
become unduly devoted to their culture and
acquisition. Yet even now it is not, and can

1

never be, wholly ignored, it being manifestly true that every social institution, whether of religion, politics, science, or art, before it could have become articulate in words or other visible expressions, must have been first speculatively conceived of and developed in the human mind. Its spirit is prophetic, and to discern what the true principles of our being are, to define our possibilities, and to forecast that which may, will, or ought to be, are its gifts and powers. Indeed, it is quite certain that no improvement or progress is possible that is not first ideally or spiritually conceived of and prophetically heralded. That is, except theory precede practice, practice is impossible—howbeit that theory without practice is but idle dreaming. Thus before the coming of the Christ the idea of the Kingdom of God on earth—of a social condition of peace and brotherhood—was merely speculative, a pure idealism, conceived of in the spirit of prophecy. The theory of gravitation, suggested to Newton's mind by the falling of an apple to the ground, could not have become an institute of science, had it not first been mentally elaborated. Nor could any constitutional system of government have been practically realized, had not the founders thereof theoretically discerned its principles and defined them in its written constitution. In short, every invention, discovery, structure, or creation of human or divine art, must have been subjectively discerned before it could have been objectively realized.

But, as we have indicated, idealism—walking by faith and not by sight (2 Cor. 5: 7), which studies the evidences of things unseen (Heb. 11: 1) that it may develop better outward conditions of life, may be so limited and applied to the development of material interests as to become merely sensual in character—so sensual in fact that the higher interests of our social and spiritual nature may come to be regarded as of little or no importance. Hence, when we say that speculative philosophy has fallen into disrepute, we do not mean that it has ceased to exist—for that is impossible even in a condition of perfect savagery, the faculty of idealization being innate in human nature—but that in this age, in which men have come to think they live by bread alone, it is limited, debased, and perverted to merely sensual uses in the conditions of time and space—in which case our higher and limitless possibilities of social and spiritual improvement are at the best but dimly discerned, and often deemed impossible of realization. Necessarily in our imperfection we see through a glass darkly, and when heavenly ideals are presented to our minds they seem shadowy and unreal, and we are little conscious of their prophetic character—of the promises and opportunities presented therein of increase in the riches of life, wisdom, and power.

We have entitled this work " An Institute of Christian Sociology." We believe our Christian faith to be an idealistic conception of inspired prophecy of a social condition of universal peace and brotherhood, originally and practically applied by Jesus the Christ in the establishment of his Church. We are not seeking to develop a new and original theory of our own, but rather to define and apply one that has already been partially developed, but in this materialistic age is but dimly discerned. Although its principles as illustrated in the Old and New Testament Scriptures are still retained in the congregations of the Church, congregations still professedly Christian, they are but little understood or practiced.

The requisite to a clear understanding of Christian Sociology is an accurate definition, first, of its primary principles of which it is predicated, as is that also of every other useful and lasting institution; and second, of the right methods by which such principles are pratically applied to the solution of all social problems. We shall not, however, attempt an exposition of such principles any farther than they pertain to our immediate subject, or are essential to the discrimination of the theories of Christian sociology from others which may apparently or really be in conflict therewith.

We shall, therefore, assume it to be true that GOD IS—not *a* God; for if HE IS, He Is in the fullest sense *Personal* and *Infinite*. The I AM (Ex. 3: 14), comprehensive of all persons and things, and cannot be simply *a* being among many beings, but *Being Itself*, the All in All (1 Cor. 12: 6; 15: 28), the To Be of all beings, and the To Do of all creations and activities (Acts 17: 28). Moreover, He is social Being—not *a* social being, but Social Being Itself, of whom and in whom every being that exists is a social being. That is, being the One and sole Reality, all existing things are realizations thereof. Thus we may reason: I think, therefore I exist; I exist, therefore GOD IS.

We shall further assume that the primary elements or principles on which all right social institutions are based, though differing from each other and limitless in number, are harmonious with each other, essential to the being of

each other, and together constitute the Unity
of Being.

But as every unity must be the union of two
or more things, we assume that the Unity of
Infinite Being consists in the union of three
groups of primary elements or principles,
namely: the elements of Substance, the elements of Nature, and the elements of Art.

Substance is the source of all substantives;
and substantives are articulations or expressions of Substance, either to our physical or
mental perceptions, whereby we may see and
possess in objective forms all subjective realities
(Acts 14: 17; Rom. 1: 20; Heb. 11: 3). Thus
the human body is a substantive, and is not only
an outward and visible expression of our inward
and personal being, but also a habitation of the
spirit and a medium of activities in this world.
In fact, without Substance it would be impossible to articulate Nature or Art, or even to
conceive ideas or images of thought. All right
social institutions, objectively made manifest,
as is Christian faith in the Church of Christ
(Heb. 11: 1), are substantives—expressions in
his Substance of God's social Nature and Art.
Unless our ideas of social culture are derived
from him, they cannot be expressed in his Substance, or practically applied to the improve-

ment of society, being, as are all other false and deceptive things, evolved from the corrupt use and perversion of our natural gifts.

Nature comprehends the primary elements of Being which determine, and are, the character and quality of Being, of all things rightly existing therein, and their proper conditions and relations. These elements constitute the laws of Being, which, though not the ultimate sources of authority—not authority itself—express authority. Thus as the human body, which expresses the substance or personality, is not the substance or personality, but only the expression thereof, so while the natural principles of Being are expressed in natural laws, natural laws are not the natural principles or personality of Being, but only the expression thereof. Yet neither substance nor nature is derived, but both are original elements of uncreated Being—were in the beginning with Being, and are Being.

The principles of Art are the original sources of all authority, and constitute, in conjunction with Substance and Nature, the divine Personality. From them we derive all mental faculties—will, volition, conscience, reason, memory, forethought, sensation, as also all original powers of reflection and construction.

They are also the sources of motion and life, whereby, being in conjunction with Substance and Nature, and in absolute harmony therewith, as a healthy mind with a healthy body, all things become instinct with intelligence, and represent in all their organisms and activities the presence and inspiration of art.

Now, in an objective sense, Nature as distinguished from Art is popularly supposed to be the work of God as distinguished from that of man. It is conceded, however, that true art is in harmony with nature, is a copy of nature, or an ideal conception which, though not yet articulate in visible forms, is yet a possibility of natural development. If this be true—if true art be necessarily in harmony with nature, and may be naturally developed—the one cannot be limited to the works of man, nor the other to the works of God.

If man be in God's image (Gen. 1 : 26), he must be, when perfect, in all things as God Is; his works as God's works. Hence, if in a subjective sense there is art in man, so must it be also in God; and the same is true of nature. Both are in the being of God, as in that of perfect man, intrinsic and harmonious differences, as matter and mind, body and soul. Both have been from eternity in one Being, in one Personal

Unity; and as it would be absurd to suppose God created himself, we must conclude that subjective Art and Nature in him are his attributes, coeternal in him. He did not originate subjective Art, which includes his own original powers of consciousness and will; nor Nature, which is the original character and quality of Being. Like our own, his Being is both subjective and outwardly expressed in objective existences, active and passive, voluntary and involuntary. In short, if man be the offspring of God, God is the Original Man, differing from perfect man only in degree; and true art and nature are alike in the being of each, and are identical, though one person differs from another in individuality as parent from child, or as in comprehensions and powers the infinite differs from the finite.

It is also generally supposed that natural laws and all objects of nature are the creations of God; which is true, if by creation we mean the outward expression of his Nature and Art, but is erroneous if we mean thereby that he originated the sources of natural laws and objects of nature; for this would be to suppose he originated himself. God is himself Substance, Nature, and Art, and these are eternal in him. Being Infinite and comprehensive of all

things, he does not originate anything outside
of himself, for if he did he would originate
something from nothing, which is absurd.   Yet
while he originates no thing he creates all
things, causes them to grow (*creare*), evolves,
constructs and develops them.   That is, he expresses his Nature in natural objects, and his
Art in natural works.   Hence God is not natural objects nor natural works, but these are
the revelations or expressions of God, and exist
of him and in him.   But while nature and art
are ever in perfect harmony, so that what are
natural are ideal, and what are ideal are also
natural, they are always more or less at vari-
ance in corrupt and sinful men.

Subjective Art in the Being of God is the
limitless power of the divine will in the evolution and development in substantive forms of
pure ideals conceived of the divine Consciousness; and Substance and Nature are the medium and means of such development.   Thus
the creation from the original elements of Substance of a beautiful world in accordance with
the laws of Nature was the work of divine Art
—the materialization of God's ideal.   So also
his efforts to redeem the social world from its
chaotic and sinful conditions—to bring order
out of chaos, freedom from bondage, right from

wrong, joy from sorrow, beauty from ashes, heaven from hell—are the evidences and illustrations of his power to evolve and develop that which should be from that which is, and to direct and control all social interests according to his will (Isa. 61: 1-4).

Nature in itself is passive, but in unity with art is put in motion and produces endless chains of causes and effects—just as the organs of the human body are put in motion by the presence of the spirit,—whereby the purposes of art are fulfilled instinctively and unconsciously to itself therein ; and the methods by which such purposes are fulfilled are what we call the laws of nature. And as every effect must correspond with its cause, even as reasonableness must correspond with reason, and as the divine consciousness and will are the original causes of natural activities, the laws of nature must be reasonable and just. They are God's ways, which, being absolutely right, know no variableness, neither shadow of turning (Jas. 1: 17).

In this connection we can understand the difference between the natural law of evolution and the special providence of God, the one being passive and involuntary—the mechanical operation of natural laws established from

eternity, which produces natural, that is reasonable, causes and effects,—and the other im-
passioned and voluntary, the overruling and
directing, the working out by means of natural
laws the ideal conceptions, plans, and purposes
of the divine mind. As Nature and Art are
intrinsic and harmonious differences in the
Being of God, so are evolution and providence
in respect to all things which exist therein.
They are never in conflict, while one is the con-
tinuous and the inevitable sequence of prece-
dent conditions, and the other wholly a matter
of volition. As in man, so is there in God the
power to develop his ideals—to avail himself
of natural laws to work out his special plans
and purposes. That is, while the evolution of
like from like, which we may call natural selec-
tion,—whereby the continuity and order of
things are secured, each thing perpetuating
itself in accordance with original and eternally
established principles,—is a law of Being which
knows no variableness, neither shadow of turning, there are necessarily involved therewith
spiritual forces which have been from eternity,
and which established this law, whereby new
and improved natural conditions may be secured. Nature and Art are naturally involved,
so that while natural laws are invariable in op-

eration, that which is evolved thereby is always previously designed, and may vary in accordance with the plans and purposes of Art. Thus a natural wilderness will naturally reproduce itself, and will always remain a wilderness with no improvement or change, and chaos will produce chaos, except by the intervention of art there be developed therefrom a cultured landscape or a beautiful world. Nature has no purpose in itself but to exist as it is, but when joined with art, as it must necessarily be, both being in one Being, it represents the purposes of art, and may produce unlimited variations and improvements. As is a human being in a finite sense, so is God in an infinite sense able to construct whatever he will—not, however, contrary to natural laws, but by means of, and in accordance with, such laws. Thus a sinful man may, without destroying his nature, become so improved in nature as to become a righteous man.

As we become more and more conscious by the education and development of our faculties, of higher and purer sources of life and happiness, we naturally strive for their realization. The conscience becomes increasingly conscious of higher ideals, purer emotions and sympathies, and the will strives to make them real—

to express in substantive forms that which otherwise were merely fanciful. New aspirations are awakened and seek expression in our outward surroundings, that which is outward and visible may be in harmony with that which is inward and spiritual—that which now is with that which may and ought to be.

The natural order, therefore, whereby from things past, things present have been evolved, and from things present, things to come will be made to appear, is not, as many suppose, indicative of a lack of intelligence and design in Being; but on the contrary all fixed laws reveal a character, plan, and purpose, and so far from limiting the Supreme Intelligence, denote an unlimited power of volition and construction. As well might we suppose that, because we are subject to natural laws, we have no power to will, create, or construct anything at all, or to improve our condition, as that the natural law of evolution—which simply means that like produces like, or that every effect is a rational sequence of its cause—renders it impossible that there should be an overruling providence. Law, so far from limiting possibilities, or freedom of action and volition, is the source and medium thereof, so that without fixed principles of law and order there would be no authority or power at all, law being the expression of conscience and volition. Though it is impossible to suppose the Infinite Mind should be capricious, or that from eternity having established natural laws it should now annul them, we must yet believe that by these laws are all things possible, and that by means of, and in harmony therewith, it is able to fulfill all its purposes.

But it is queried how, if there be an overruling providence, sin, injustice, and undeserved suffering should be permitted to exist in the world. But this questioning arises from our separating Nature and Art from each other, whereas they are mutually involved, so that the expression of one is also that of the other, and each must be harmonious with the other—so that if we have corrupted our art, our nature will necessarily be also corrupt. A like difficulty arises from separating the ideas of the natural and supernatural from each other; for if we suppose that the supernatural is contrary to the natural, and has no respect to natural laws, we are entertaining an absurdity—all laws, natural or spiritual, being ordained of God, and it being impossible to suppose that he would or could thwart his own purposes and decrees. He may suffer the tares to grow un-

til the harvest, lest in rooting them up the good
wheat be rooted up also, but they will certainly
be destroyed at last.   It is man, not God, that
permits oppressive and unjust social conditions
to exist; for as God has imparted his own free
will to man—for otherwise man could not
exist, could not be a man without having a will
of his own as God has—he could not compel a
sinful human being to be righteous, contrary to
its own will; and as all men are more or less
selfish, he could not instantly blot out iniquity
without blotting out the whole human race.
The common idea that God can do anything
we can conceive of, however absurd, is a
fallacy; for in fact—and for the very reason
that he is omnipotent, all-wise, and absolutely
just and perfect—he cannot do a great many
things that are possible to finite, foolish, unjust
and sinful men.   Necessarily, therefore, in a
sinful world, the just will unjustly suffer for
the unjust—not by God's permission, for he
does not and will not permit injustice cease-
lessly to endure—it proving ultimately true in
all cases, as in the example of the Christ, that
those who are persecuted for righteousness' sake
are really blessed thereby (Matt. 5 : 10 ; Rom. 8 :
18, 28).

The Infinite Perfection—the original and

perfect Man—is of all men the standard absolute of righteousness : and unless we rule our
theories and works by this standard—unless
in our substance, nature, and art, in body, mind,
and spirit, we are in unity with God, our work
is unlawful, irrational, unjust, vain, and sinful,
and can only evolve social conditions of poverty and distress. If, for example, we go on in
sin that grace may abound (Rom. 6 : 1); strive
to right wrong by wrong; seek justification by
injustice; secure or hold riches by making
others poor; seek freedom by enslaving others;
or knowledge and refinement by making others
ignorant and brutal;—in short if our theory
and practice are not in harmony with the
divine Art and Nature, we deceive ourselves,
pervert and degrade our gifts of God, and involve our social being in otherwise needless
poverty and distress.

It is plain, therefore, that except we improve
our art our social redemption is impossible.
There must be first a true theory of reform, an
ideal conception of better social relations and
conditions, and this must be practically applied
to the proper adjustment and development
thereof. Such reform, however, cannot come by
observation (Luke 17 : 20)—by simply folding
our hands, and waiting for its development by

the natural laws of evolution; for our nature is itself perverted, and as nature evolves like from like, it cannot in itself evolve from corrupt social conditions those which are just. All reform must come by art, by improvement of our conscience and will—by ideal conceptions imparted by the direct inspiration of the Spirit of God, and practically applied to the reformation of our present unnatural and corrupt social life.   ·

Although subject ever to natural laws, we yet possess such powers of conscience and volition that we may limitlessly improve in all things that pertain to our physical, mental, and spiritual well-being. Without such ideal conceptions derived from the inspirations of God —his consciousness and will working upon our conscience and will—we are blinded by our sin and selfishness, and grope our way in darkness. There must be a mark set before us, to which, forgetting the things behind, we are constantly pressing forward (Phil. 3: 14); there must be prophecy and promise; there must be a right social theory—a practical faith in our limitless possibilities of improvement in the limitless power of an omnipotent and loving Father. From him must be derived our personal consciousness of our ability to develop and perfect our manhood. Being sinful, and yet conscious that we are not totally depraved, we may increase in righteousness; being weak, we may yet limitlessly increase in physical, mental and spiritual power; being poor and blind and miserable, yet possessed in some degree of every faculty of God, we may increase in his boundless riches, in his infinite comprehensions of knowledge, and in his exhaustless sources of happiness. For as he is the Infinite and Absolute, and as we are of and in him—are his offspring, sons and heirs of his boundless riches— all things may be ours, and we may receive of him in limitless measure (1 Cor. 3 : 22). Every limit, indeed, is a positive evidence of an illimitable, as is every drop of water of an ocean ; every particle of dust, of a world; every finite being, of Infinite Being; every imperfection, of an absolute Perfection; every good thing we enjoy, of limitless sources of enjoyment; every social privilege, of boundless freedom ; every life, of boundless life,—for no part of being, however small, can become separated from the infinite All, from which it is derived.

The goal of humanity, of an individual, family, or nation, is its absolute perfection, in which there is perfect unity of the human with the divine Substance, Nature, and Art; and if this be realized and steadily pursued, there will be an immediate, great, and rapid increase in social freedom and enjoyment.

But this ideal conception of our possibilities of social improvement, developed of our faith in the Infinite and Absolute Perfection, would be practically useless, inspiring only unsatisfied longings, unless accompanied with a clear and definite conception of the practical methods by which it can be realized. We may believe in the reality of things which our eyes have not seen, nor ears heard, neither have yet entered into our hearts—may, indeed, have certainty in our minds of their existence, and that they are possibilities of our social life, and yet have no knowledge of the methods by which they may be practically realized. Thus we may feel sure that there might be a social condition of perfect liberty, and may picture in fancy such condition, and yet be utterly blind to the way in which it may become an actual experience,— may even regard it as impossible of attainment in this life. But if, as we believe, the moral law, known as the Ten Commandments, is a full and complete definition of social rights and obligations, and if Jesus the Christ be an example of perfected humanity, and his gospel the fulfillment of the law in love, we have pre-

sented to us in all essential details the true and
practical theory of social redemption in the
perfection of human nature and art. Assuming this to be true, all that is necessary to the
right solution of all social problems is the
practical application of this law and gospel.
In this way we may right every wrong, and
open every prison door—and in this way only,
since it is self-evident that all social improvement must be measured by the degree of our
approximation to the ideal standard of manhood presented in the example and teaching of
the Perfect Man.

At this time great social problems are imperatively demanding solution. There have
come to pass in the progress of our culture so
great developments of conscience and volition,
that there is almost universal discontent with
the unjust and oppressive social conditions and
relations in which we live, and which we have
in part inherited from our barbarian ancestry.
This discontent has arisen from a better understanding of natural and acquired rights, and of
the limitations imposed thereon by past ignorance and present cupidity, whereby our nature
and art are perverted to sensual and selfish
uses. Our insane and almost exclusive devotion to material riches, and our reckless compe-

tition in their acquirement have resulted in the
enrichment of the few and the impoverishment
of the many; and the latter, instructed and
disciplined by their sufferings, and enlightened
by increased development and wider diffusion
of knowledge, have come to realize the enslavement they are compelled to endure, and
have rebelled against it,—although they have
as yet but little conception· of right social
theories, whereby equal social rights and privileges may be practically realized. Deeming
that others more fortunate than themselves are
their oppressors—walking by sight and not by
faith, judging by appearances and not by principles,—they conclude that if the wealth of the
favored few were forcibly taken from them and
equally divided among the masses, all would
be rich, free, and equal; whereas we can secure
social rights only to the degree we observe
social duties.

While, no doubt, the civilization of our age
is superior to any that has preceded it, yet as
every virtue gives by its perversion the opportunity of a corresponding vice, and the greater
the virtue the greater the vice developed therefrom, our great advancement in religious, political, industrial, scientific, and æsthetic culture
has been accompanied with a corresponding in-

crease in debasing and vicious parasitic growths,
whereby things that are good are perverted into
things that are evil. Hence no past age has
presented so great and so varied developments
as the present of diseases, vices, crimes, and
systems of oppression—such subtleties and refinements of cruelty. The three parasitic and
all comprehensive elements of destruction—the
Moth, Rust, and Thief (Matt. 6: 19)—have found
new and numberless opportunities of multipli-
cation in the great increase of riches and knowledge perverted to unnatural uses—to excessive
devotion to the letter to the neglect of the spirit
of natural, moral, and spiritual laws, whereby
they have become tributary to selfishness and
sensuality. Although all progress comes by the
right culture of art, whereby our nature is improved and exalted, art is merely fictitious and
degrading if in conflict with a true nature. Its
spirit, naturally idealistic and prophetic of better things, may become simply realistic and
sensual, merely formal and mechanical, judging only by appearances, and walking by sight
rather than by faith.

Believing that Christian faith, hope, and charity, evolved of the Ten Commandments, of the
example of a perfected humanity in Jesus the
Christ, and of his gospel of universal peace and

brotherhood, present the true theory of social
redemption, our effort in this study is to understand and define what this theory is, what are
the social problems it seeks to solve, and what
are the right methods by which it may be practically applied.   It is the ideal conception in the
Divine Mind, incarnated in humanity, of what
our social relations should be, of what we should
and may become—the social polity of the Kingdom of God, which he seeks to establish on
earth.   If we make this conception our own,—
if this faith of God in us becomes our faith in
ourselves, in our own possibilities of improvement,—we may rightly solve all social problems,
and go on unto perfection (Matt. 5 : 44).   Otherwise—unless we are led thereby to ideal conceptions of improved social relations, and realize
them in our outward life—the further progress
of our race is impossible.   We have plainly
reached the limit of improvement possible while
the social problems that confront us remain un-
solved.   Our nature and art are so perverted
and conflicting, and our social life and happiness are so involved therein, that unless
brought into harmonious relations, our civilization, like the many that have preceded it,
though nominally Christian, must perish.   There
must either be reform, whereby the real im-

provements of the past may be saved and utilized for further improvements, or there will be
indiscriminate destruction of our religious, educational, and political systems. Nature will
inevitably produce the rational sequences of
present conditions, and is, when our theories
and practices are in conflict with the conscience
and will of God, as necessarily destructive of
them as the wages of sin is death; but pre-
servative of them if in harmony therewith.

That reform is wiser than iconoclasm should
be plainly manifest. Evil is not positive, but
negative, and is always associated with partial
good. It is always the just evolution of perverted nature and art. There is in fact no such
thing possible in Being as pure original evil.
What is called such is a parasitic development
of diseased social life. Every evil is in some
sense right and natural, being the result of our
transgressions of the laws of God. Hence true
reform will without destruction save that which
is lost. Thus the worship of idols may be converted into that of the true God; the Church,
however corrupt, into the Kingdom of Heaven;
a government, however tyrannical, into one of
liberty, equality, and fraternity; a body or
mind, however weak or diseased, into one of
strength and health; death into life, sin into

righteousness, and even Satan into an angel of light.

Complicated and difficult as may appear the social problems that confront us, there is always a plain and simple way by which each may be rightly and practically solved. But there is only one true way—the way of God; for the infinite and absolute Perfection precludes the possibility of any other than that which approximates his Standard of righteousness. And if Jesus the Christ, as we believe, was the Perfect Man, his idealism, his theory of social redemption, must represent the divine Consciousness and Will; his Way, Truth, and Life in a perfected humanity. His wisdom, his social science, practically applied to our redemption from all suffering and oppression, is the Beautiful Gate of entrance to the Temple of God.

BOOK FIRST.

SOCIALISTIC IDEAS.

" Now Peter and John went up together into the temple at the hour of prayer, being the ninth hour."—Acts 3: 1.

PROLOGUE.

MAN is the race of men—the totality of beings of his kind; and whether as an individual, family, or nation, he exists only as one of many. One MAN is all men, and all men are one MAN. Every element or attribute of the One exists also in the other, nor could either exist without the other—the infinite Whole without its finite parts, or the finite parts without their infinite Whole—any more than father without children, or children without father.

God is the Original Man, being the original Father of all men, and all men being his offspring and in his likeness (Gen. 1: 27; Acts 17: 28, 29), in him are all elements of fatherhood, sonship, and brotherhood. Man is therefore necessarily a social being. As an individual he cannot live unto himself alone (Rom. 14: 7, 8; 2 Cor. 5: 15), but must live unto society as society must live unto God, and must sustain the relations of father, son, or brother, and in the natural order of his being all these

29

relations. He has a natural place, duty, and
right in society, and society the same in him,
to ignore which would be to ignore Being itself,
in which all things have being, the transgression of all natural and moral laws, and the destruction of all gifts naturally derived from
sonship in the universal Father. All his personal interests are necessarily identical with
those of society, and nothing he can do, or be,
or possess, exclusive of the interests of his fellow-men, or in conflict therewith, can be conducive to his own ultimate well-being. That
is, he cannot be selfish without injury to himself and others. The well-being of society is
the well-being of every individual member
thereof; and that of every individual member
that of society. And he is not only social in
nature but wholly social—all his faculties of
mind and body, as well his surroundings and
possessions being socialistic—of society, for society, and by society. His individuality, his
organic unity of body and soul, is possessed in
common with all others of his kind, all individualities being derived from, and comprehended in, the Individuality of God, being
unities of Unity. Indeed the true idea of individuality can differ from that of sociality only
as the degrees of their comprehensions differ—

the one combining all the primary elements that constitute a personality, and the other combining all personalities.

The common idea, therefore, that because one human being differs from all others in individuality, is distinct and separate from them in body, mind, and spirit, and possesses an independent conscience and will, he has no interest in or responsibility to or for others, is a fallacy. As well might one organ of the human body assert its independence of all others, as one man of all other men—all organs being united in one body, and dependent upon that body, as are all individuals in one society, all children in one family, and all citizens in one State or Nation (1 Cor. 12: 14-27). A selfish individualism is, in fact, the perversion and destruction of its own individuality—the source of all personal weakness, poverty, and decay.

Nor is the common idea true that individuality is decreased by sociality, and would be swallowed up and extinguished in an absolutely perfect community of individual interests; but on the contrary it is increased thereby, and would in a perfect community be itself perfect. As individuality is born of society, and is of the same nature, it can only be developed therein by the community of its members—of husbands and wives, parents and children, brothers and sisters, friends and neighbors—so that, the more such community is improved and strengthened, so also must be the individualities that compose it. Thus the individuality of a man or woman is increased by marriage, of parents by children, of citizens by the increased greatness of their country, and especially of the whole human race to the degree it grows in the consciousness of its own possibilities of life and power in the Kingdom of God.

What is true respecting the social nature of God and man is also true of all other beings. And as man is the highest order in this world, and all things are subject to him and for his use (Gen. 1: 26-30), the corruption of his nature must necessarily corrupt that of every other inferior order; for it plainly should be and is the law of Being—the rational and just evolution of like from like—that our environment should correspond with our social conditions—our physical and objective with our spiritual and subjective. The world we live in must be as we are—the mirror which reflects our own image. In fact we make our own world, whether a heaven or hell. Hence if we are harmonious within ourselves, so will our surroundings be which exist of us—all animals, plants, and inanimate things being congenial therewith (Job 5 . 23). When we are at peace with God and with each other, then will all things with which we live, and which grow and exist of us, be at peace with us and with each other. In the place of the thorn and briar will appear the fir and myrtle (Isa. 55 : 13), the wolf dwell with the lamb, the sucking child play on the hole of the asp, and all ideas of evil be banished from human consciousness (Rev. 21 : 4) ; for it is not possible in the nature of things, or in the mercy and wisdom of God, that that which is evil be eternally associated with that which is good—howbeit a partial evil may and must be associated with a partial good until such evil is overcome with good. Doubtless the tree of life and the tree of the knowledge of good and evil must always and everywhere for our discipline in obedience grow together—it being impossible that we should be free agents or possess anything good without the possibility of perverting it to evil, —yet we may learn to always choose the good and reject the evil (Gen. 2 : 9 ; Isa. 7 : 15 ; Ezek. 18 : 31, 32).

Now if it be true that Being is the Unity of all beings, and that as a necessary and rational sequence thereof all beings are social, mutually dependent, reciprocally giving and receiving, it is plain that to the degree any person is unsocial he is inharmonious with Being, and his nature perverted. In other words an unsocial person—one who does not give as he receives, willing to receive but unwilling to bestow—is unjust and unrighteous, and therefore sinful. Hence sin is accurately defined as unsociality; and as unsociality is selfishness, selfishness is sin. Indeed it is impossible to conceive of any practical idea of sin that is not unsocial and selfish; and we must infer that the culture of true religion and righteousness, and the realization of unity and peace are possible only through the extermination of selfishness.

Selfishness is individualism as opposed to socialism; and although our individuality is our greatest personal gift, being derived of the Individuality of God, and comprehensive of all mental and physical faculties, and all capacities for life and enjoyment, it becomes when perverted to selfish uses correspondingly weak and miserable; "for what can it profit a man if he gain the whole world and lose his own soul?" (Matt. 22: 13). Yet it is hard for selfish men to realize that the more one gains through his selfishness the more he loses, and that a selfish rich man is really naked, poor, blind, and miser-

able (Rev. 3 : 17). Nor can we wonder that it
is easier for a camel to go through the eye of a
needle than for such a man to enter the Kingdom of God (Matt. 19 : 24). Viewing all
things through selfish eyes, evil becomes to him
a seeming good, and good a seeming evil (Isa.
5 : 20); and judging simply from appearances
he becomes incapable of judging righteous
judgment (John 7 : 24). Of course unselfishness is paradoxical to selfish men, and is in fact
contradictory and absurd in a depraved social
condition which is itself contrary to the natural
order of Being. Thus a selfish social order
renders it necessary for each member thereof to
look out for himself, save himself if he can
from beggary and starvation, and if possible
acquire, whether honestly or dishonestly, such
independence of riches as will not only save
him from want, but confer upon him special
social powers and privileges. No doubt it is
wise to regard all communistic ideas as fanatical, impracticable, and absurd in the present
condition of society—that is, wise in a selfish
sense for selfish men. If we regard unselfishness unwise and impracticable, then is it unwise and impracticable to us, for as a man
thinketh in his heart so is he (Prov. 23: 7).
If we cannot understand truth because it is the

truth (John 8 : 45), then is falsehood true to
us, sin righteousness, and selfishness charity.
If we love the god of this world more than the
God of the heavenly world, then is this world
heaven to us, and heaven is hell. But if we
permit ourselves to be so blinded as to deem
unselfishness impracticable and unwise—the
social polity of the Kingdom of God impossible
in the present condition of the world—not realizing that this present condition exists
through our selfishness, or that, if we cease
ourselves to be selfish, then unselfishness would
become practicable—our wisdom is but foolishness with God (1 Cor. 3: 19). In fact our
selfish wisdom is but a snare (Ps. 9: 16; 1
Tim. 6: 9)—like the gallows Haman erected,
an instrument of our own destruction. There
is not a word of evil import in human speech
that is not the expression of selfishness, nor an
evil thought, impulse, or desire that is not inspired thereby. Hence our only possible
salvation is in the extermination of selfishness; for it is manifestly impossible that a
selfish person should be admitted to the Kingdom of God, or that the Kingdom of God
should be introduced into this world except to
the degree we become unselfish. And the only
possible way in which selfishness can be exter-

minated is by the establishment of right social relations between men, whereby the best interests of each will be recognized as the best interests of all.

PART I.

THE SOCIALISTIC IDEA OF RELIGION.

SUBJECTIVE religion is the conscience of our mutual obligations and of the principles, laws, and necessities upon which such obligations are based. Objective it is in its application to the outward adjustment of social relations, and the culture of social interests in accordance with such principles, laws or necessities. Its primary meaning—derived from the Latin *religere* or *religare*, to bind back or collect together—is unity of God and Man, and of man and man, in one family, society, or nation. And as man is naturally and necessarily a social being, its idea—inseparable from his nature—is an instinctive conception in the mind of each individual of social duty. Its motive is love; and as every faculty of our minds is the ability to love that of which it has power to conceive, whether of a physical or spiritual entity, love is in a finite sense of man, and is man, as it is in a limitless sense of God, and is God (1 John 4: 8), and is the bond of union and mutual sympathy whereby all persons are bound together in harmonious relations. Hence, religion is the theory and practice of love in all social relations—as of God and man, of husband and wife, of parent and child, of brother and sister, and of friends, neighbors, and citizens. It is the first conscience of our infancy, whereby we recognize our union with others and our dependence upon them; and from this are evolved all our ideas of authorities, obligations, rights, and opportunities. Historically this bond of union is traced back through each person's ancestry to the original founder of his race, extends down to his offspring, and collaterally to brothers and sisters and their descendants, thus binding him to all others of his family or race. Necessarily its inception in humanity was in the consciousness of the first man of his relations with God, and through him was naturally transmitted to his descendants. But as men multiplied and became widely separated in time and space and by diverse habits of life, the original idea became more or less obscured, and its methods of culture diversified according to the degrees of intelligence developed in the various families and nations; yet in no case has it been entirely obliterated from the human conscience, nor is it possible that it should be, being, as it is, naturally evolved. Strictly speaking there can be no society without religion, as there can be no religion without society—without the mutual recognition by the members thereof of a bond of union whereby are imposed obligations of obedience to just authority, and of respect for each other's rights and interests. Whether defined as natural or revealed religion,—and the two are one and the same in principle, it being manifestly true that there can be but one true religion, as there is but one true God—it is always and necessarily social. As called " natural," religion is the expression of our natural instincts which teach our responsibilities to God and our fellow-men ; as called " revealed," it is an institution of divine art inspired in the human conscience, teaching the same or similar obligations.

It is impossible, therefore, to be socialists in any true sense except we be also in a like sense religious ; or to be religious except we be also socialists. In fact true religion is true socialism, and there can be no other—that which, in recognition of the supreme authority of God in the regulation of our relations with him and with each other, is the practical culture of all virtues. And we may safely assert that the progress of mankind in the culture of true religion exactly measures, and is coincident with, its right social culture ; and if wrong or oppression of any kind exists, it is the certain evidence that our religion is in a like degree false, corrupt, or imperfectly applied.   Hence, it is plainly futile to attempt to reform society without religion ; for if without right social principles the wronged and oppressed resort to brute force only, and in defiance of religious obligations set up their own authority as supreme in the regulation of social interests and relations, they would themselves become oppressors.   As nature cannot reform itself, there must be the intervention of art, in which only is there a sense of justice and mercy, in order to develop social improvement; and art cannot be limited simply to the exercise of brute force, although when rightly and intelligently directed by unselfish motives, brute force, being a natural force, may be utilized by a true art.

It is plain, therefore, that there must be a right theory of religion, or all efforts to promote social reform will but end in social chaos; and this theory must be inspired of the consciousness of God in the conscience of humanity.   Socialism can only be another name

for fanaticism, if it be not the development in
our social life of the heavenly ideal. There
must be an improved sense of right or there can
be no practical increase of righteousness; but if
our religion be of God, and properly cultured
and applied, social progress and reform are its
natural developments.

Peter and John were religious men—they
went up into the temple at the hour of prayer.
They recognized their obligations to God and
their fellow-men. They did not withdraw
themselves from the multitude that thronged
in at the Beautiful Gate of the temple at the
hour of prayer, although their ideas of religion
were vastly higher than those of other men,
with whose prayers to God they mingled their
own supplications. There could be no greater
exhibition of selfishness than, when one conscious of his superior gifts and possessions,
natural or acquired, withholds himself from
contact with others less favored—thus depriv-
ing them of the social advantage they might
otherwise derive from his example and teaching.

Doubtless one of the greatest hindrances to
the progress of true sociology is that the oppressed classes of society, while they make little effort to redress their wrongs in God's ap-

pointed way, devote themselves to personal resentments and hostilities, whereby they injure
themselves more than their oppressors, and by
their own acts the more enslave themselves.
To cherish a sense of injury—simply nursing
our grievances—renders it the more difficult for
others to help us, or for us to help ourselves,
and betrays a spirit directly opposed to the
principles of true religion, which require us to
love our enemies.   This love, however, is not
simply an emotional impulse, not merely sensual
or sentimental, but such a sense of what is wise,
just, and merciful as leads us to do unto others
as we would they should do unto us.   There is
always a way by which we may right our
wrongs without wronging others; to obtain
justice and mercy without being ourselves
unjust and unmerciful.   "Be ye, therefore,
wise as serpents and harmless as doves" (Matt.
10: 16).

While, therefore, Peter and John knew that
the rulers of the people with whom they joined
in worship were hypocrites, a generation of
vipers, who shut up the Kingdom of Heaven'
against men, devoured widows' houses, and for
pretense made long prayers, they yet united
with them in the public devotions, and partook
with them of the bitter herbs and unleavened

bread of their fastings.   As the temple was the
house of God, they would not voluntarily permit themselves to be debarred from its privileges by the hypocrisies of those who had made
it a den of thieves.   They did not judge its religion by the men who professed it, nor did they
reject it for the corruptions and perversions to
which it had been subjected, but as true socialists and reformers they cherished it as the embodiment of the essential and fundamental
elements of progress, without which social improvement was impossible.   So far from cherish-
ing any personal resentments, or indulging in
morbid reflections, they were intent only on
promoting the true interests of all men without
respect to class prejudices or unjust distinctions
of any kind.   They were moved only by the
spirit of love and sympathy that had caused
their Master to weep over Jerusalem, and had
wrung from him in his agony tears and bloody
sweat.   The   incorrigible   bigotry   and   self-
righteousness of the Pharisees, the sceptic conceit of the Sadducees, the selfish and heartless
arrogance of the affluent, and the sincerely
blind ignorance and superstition of the common
people, though regarded with the utmost aversion, excited no personal resentment, but on the
contrary personal compassion, regarding them

as personal infirmities and as the self-inflicted
penalties resulting from transgressions in spirit
of the social laws of God. Otherwise—as is true
of many who profess Christianity—they would
have made no efforts and sacrifices for the redemption of the world from social oppression,
but deeming themselves secure of salvation in
their own personal righteousness would have
sought refuge from persecution in the obscurity
of their humble calling as fishermen on the
shores of Galilee. Moreover, as social beings
they knew they were personally responsible to
God for the social conditions of others as well
as their own; for the wrong, ignorance, and oppression that then existed—even for the bigotry
and hypocrisy of the Pharisees and Sadducees.
No person can avoid personal responsibility by
indifference—for the errors and sufferings of the
world by hiding himself from the world; for
the corruptions and perversions of religion by
ceasing to be religious. Such a course would
be simply suicidal, the destruction of one's own
social nature.

As true religion represents the conscience and
will of God in the right adjustment of social relations, we are, if irreligious, living in rebellion
to his authority. It is not enough that one
should be in his private character what he

should be; for having also a social character
he is required to make that also what it should
be—which is impossible to irreligion; for religion, being the natural bond of union, requires
all to live in recognition and promotion of each
other's rights and interests. Nor is it enough
that one should be religious simply in a popular
sense, if that be a corruption of the natural and
original sense.

The spirit, therefore, that animated Peter and
John, when they went up into the temple to
pray, was that of reconciliation of man with
God, and of man with man. They were not
blind bigots, liberal hypocrites, nor sincerely
ignorant devotees. They did not believe that
the murderers of their Master were so utterly depraved that they were past all possibility of redemption from the awful thralldom of guilt and
social suffering in which they were involved,
but that some at least might be brought to repentance, and that ultimately society might attain perfect unity and harmony in the consciousness and will of God.

Such was their social ideal, their dream and
prophecy of better things to come, that had
been inspired in their minds by the teachings
and example of their Master, in which they so
firmly believed and trusted that they had no

hesitation in devoting their lives to its realization in social life. Corrupt as the religion of the Jewish people had become, they knew that its original principles were true and practical, and represented the universal brotherhood of man, and that only by holding fast thereto was social redemption possible. · They were reformers, not iconoclasts. Even the zeal of the Pharisees (Rom. 10 : 2), though not according to knowledge, and blinded by obdurate bigotry and worldliness, might be transformed by the renewing of their minds into a zeal of God, an enthusiastic devotion to him in the love of truth and righteousness; the sceptic liberality of the Sadducees, though rendering them hypocrites, might be converted into an enlightened and catholic spirit; and the sincere but ignorant superstition of the common people might become, when enlightened, an earnest aspiration for a higher culture in the freedom and knowledge of God. While in spirit the religion of the day was utterly repugnant to them, they yet believed it to have come originally from God, and, like those who had corrupted it, capable of reformation. They believed in prayer—in the culture of human aspirations whereby we may learn not only what we ought to strive for, but also may have ability to at-

tain. But while they prayed in the spirit of
humility and charity, those who knelt beside
them prayed in the spirit of worldly pride and
selfishness. They hungered after righteousness, seeking in the consciousness of their own
infirmities, and in compassion for the sufferings
of their fellow-men, their own personal exaltation in the exaltation of the whole human family, while others who thronged in at the Beau-
ful Gate were intent chiefly upon the promotion
of their own private and selfish interests.

Now in our day, although the religious conscience of society is greatly improved from what
it was when Peter and John went up into the
temple at the hour of prayer, it is yet very
far from the practical realization of their social
ideal. Religion is still more in the letter than
in the spirit. The bigoted leaven of the Pharisees, the liberal hypocrisy of the Sadducees,
and the sincerely ignorant superstition of the
masses, are yet potent influences in our social
life, and vitiate our religious faith. In fact religion is still so corrupt, so perverted in nature
and art, that many sincere and earnest reformers have come to regard it as a stumbling block,
a rock of offence in the progress of social redemption, an ally of oppression and a foe to the
rights and liberties of man. Impatient of its

restraints, those who are conscious of social oppression are prone to resort to other and some-
times violent methods of reform. New social
theories have been developed, whereby liberty,
equality, and fraternity, are sought to be attained without its aid, and in some of which
there is even no recognition of God.

All of these theories, however, are necessarily
untrue and impracticable in the present, or indeed in any possible social condition, for any
theory which ignores religion ignores the essential principles of our social well-being. Any
that arrays one class against another in interests—the poor against the rich, the employee
against his employer, or the reverse—however
great the wrongs one class suffers from another
—is plainly contrary to social unity, and practically tends to social chaos and the destruction
of human obligations and rights. But as every
theory must and will inevitably fail that is not
religious, being in conflict with the consciousness and will of God, so too, will every religious theory fail, if not practically applied both
in letter and spirit—in which case it may not
only be utterly useless, but also positively inimical to our social well-being—being incapable
of practical effort or of human sympathy; a
form of godliness, but denying the power

thereof (2 Tim. 3 : 5); nominally Christian, but really a demoniac full of the evil spirits of worldliness, bigotry, intolerance, selfishness, and superstition.

PART II.

THE temple at Jerusalem represented the religious culture of the Jewish people, a family that dated its origin from the beginning of the historic period of our race; and this culture, though very much corrupted when Peter and John went up thereto at the hour of prayer, was no doubt coeval with the existence of the family. Whether, as was supposed by the people, and as Peter and John doubtless believed, it was a special revelation of God, or a natural evolution and development, it is not necessary to affirm or deny; but that it was true religion we do not hesitate to assert. Assuming, as we have, that there is one only living and true God, and that in him are all primary elements of Being—of Substance, Nature, and Art, which are the limitless sources of all revelation, character, and construction—natural differs from revealed religion only as our uncultured intuitions differ from our cultured, the one being evolved of our nature only, and the other also

51

of our art specially inspired of the Divine
Conscience, whereby our nature is improved,
the gifts of prophecy imparted, higher ideals of
life conceived, and we are in spirit quickened to
increased aspirations for knowledge, power, life,
and happiness.

Like all things else, whether naturally or artificially evolved, religion must have successive
stages of development, which may be defined
under three heads :—the intuitive, in which men
are directed and controlled by the social instincts of their nature, and with little or no reflection ; the disciplinary, in which social obligations are intellectually recognized, defined,
and enforced ; and the spiritual, in which men
through the enlightenment of their conscience
and the improvement of their nature are no
longer subject to discipline, but voluntarily fulfill in love that which otherwise they are con-
strained to do only by compulsion. As com-
monly understood, these are the natural, the
moral, and the spiritual stages of religious development.

The Temple represented the second or moral
stage, wherein social obligations are consciously
recognized, defined, and classified, in what is
called the Moral Law. This law, though partially developed in the religions of all people

who have made any advancement in social culture beyond their natural instincts, has never been fully and systematically defined by any except the Abrahamic family, which, in remote times, and in an age of seemingly little consciousness, embodied all the primary and essential principles of morality in what are known as the Ten Commandments. How this family could have so thoroughly analyzed man's social nature, and so accurately defined its moral obligations, in the rude state of its culture, which the wisest philosophers among the most cultured people of subsequent times have been unable to do, we cannot explain, except it were, as asserted in the ancient traditions of the family, by a special revelation of God. But however that may be, we may assume that it is what it purports to be, since it is now universally accepted as such, and no critic has been able to detect any error or omission therein, or suggest any addition or qualification. It appears absolutely faultless and complete.

The First Article of this code affirms the being of one only living and true God as the sole and ultimate source of all personal and social obligations and rights. "Thou shalt have no other Gods before me," is not, however, an arbitrary and tyrannical assertion of authority, but the enunciation and teaching of the primary and fundamental principle of all true philosophy, upon which our social improvement and well-being depend; for unless there were ultimate and absolute authority there could not be intrinsic truths, rights, or obligations, and all conceptions of goodness, happiness, or beauty would be wholly fanciful and fictitious. By ultimate and absolute we mean that which is and of the Infinite, which has no beginning nor ending, and in its ceaseless continuity represents a perfect and invariable standard of whatever is, may, must, and ought to be. And this idea of the absolute is necessarily of an Infinite Person; for otherwise the idea of absolute right could not exist in our personal conscience. Except the source of our personal conscience were itself personally conscious it could not confer personal conscience. Nor could it confer personal rights except it were personally capable of apprehending what righteousness is.

Now the idea of an Infinite Person from whom our rights are derived, and by whom our obligations are imposed, is necessarily communistic, being the consciousness of our dependence, and reliance upon higher powers, wherein it is not possible for us to live unto ourselves alone; and in this consciousness is our first conception of religion, of social rights and opportunities conferred, and of corresponding obligations and duties imposed thereby. As is the infant's first recognition of the authority of its parents, of its dependence upon them, and of the unity of its interests with theirs, so is man's first recognition of his relations with God. Denial of such relations in anything we do or neglect to do is the beginning of transgression and the origin of sin. If, therefore, we seek to cultivate and improve our social conditions, we must base our social philosophy upon this first and fundamental principle of the moral law, that there is one only living and true God, in whose supreme Consciousness and Will originate all social rights, duties, and authorities.

The Second Article affirms the sinfulness of idolatry—defined as the making unto ourselves, as an object of worship, any graven image or likeness of any existing thing in heaven above, in the earth beneath, or in the water under the earth.

Making to ourselves, as an object of worship, any image or likeness of any existing thing, is either constructing such image or likeness, or converting from its natural use any existing

thing. Thus the construction of a golden calf
for an object of worship, or the converting of a
living calf into such object, is making to ourselves an idol. And as everything in heaven
above, or in the earth beneath, or in the water .
under the earth—whether of man's or of God's
creation—may in this way become an idol,
every good gift we receive or rightfully acquire, if we bow down to it and worship it,
may be perverted to evil. True worship is the
culture of true religion—of the love of God and
our fellow-men—but the one may be perverted
into the culture of false religion, and the other
into the self-love which is disobedience to God
and hatred of our fellow-men. All things that
exist—that is, are made manifest—exist of and
in the Being of God, and are his creatures, and
to worship the creature rather than the Creator
(Rom. 1: 25) reverses the natural order of worship, and debases the character and quality of
our natural life. And as our natural life is our
religious life, derived from its unity with the
life of God, and lived in harmony with his conscience and will, we cannot be religious—harmoniously united with God and each other—if
we subject ourselves to inferior things, whether
such subjection be by the worship of an inferior
faculty or desire in body or mind—which is

sensuality, or of our whole being to an inferior being—which is personal thralldom.

There is a natural and just order of priority —in all true relations (Rom. 13: 7), each thing that exists being dependent upon a superior, and though each has merits and rights in its degree, and is worthy of just consideration and respect, it is not to be made equal to that which is superior to itself (John 8: 54). Age, position, culture, abilities, riches in all things of intrinsic value, if lawfully acquired and used for unselfish purposes, are entitled to respect, yet if worshipped as supreme, or as superior to better things, such worship is idolatry. True worship is the recognition of merits in their natural order, and leads up to the recognition of God as the supreme source of all merits, that is of whom all merits exist. Merit is authority, and the proper recognition of authority is obedience, and the culture of obedience is true worship.

Though we profess to believe in the one only living and true God, yet worship him not in spirit and in truth, not having a true idea of what he is, that is, what his merits are, we are manifestly idolaters. In this way even God may become to us only an idol, being in our conception of him converted into an inferior being—our faith merely a sectarian creed, fetish, or shibboleth of man's device, our hope only a selfish aspiration to save ourself, and our charity only a matter of almsgiving.

Whether we engrave a fancied image of God in wood or stone, or draft theological symbols representing our own fanciful, eccentric, bigoted, and superstitious ideas of him, we are equally idolaters—having "changed the glory of the incorruptible God into an image made like to corruptible man" (Rom. 1: 23). If we are bigoted or superstitious, selfish, not willing to give as we receive, uncharitable, not willing to share equally with others in our opportunities, so is the God we worship. "Know ye not that to whom ye yield yourselves servants to obey, his servants ye are to whom ye obey, whether of sin unto death or of obedience unto righteousness?" (Ro. 6: 16).

What is true of God is also true of his religion—it may become to us practically only a worship of idols—its Temple or Church only a nursery of superstitions—not of God, but of selfish, unloving, world-minded men. To suppose that religion is only a matter of rites and ceremonies, of sensations and sentimentalisms, and not a culture of eternal principles of unity between God and man, and man and man, is to make such culture only a worship of false gods. As a man is as he thinketh in his heart (Prov. 23 : 7), so is he, if he be a worshipper of the God of this world (2 Cor. 4 : 4), an idolater, even if he calls the one only living and true God his God. Doubtless there is no greater idolatry than that which is cloaked under the image or likeness of true religion. Thus the Temple of God became a den of thieves who worshipped Mammon rather than God (Matt. 6 : 24). Anti-christ is called the Christ (1 John 2 : 18) ; the friendship of the world, friendship with God (James 4 : 4) ; a world-minded congregation, a church—which is falling down and worshipping Satan (Rev. 2 : 9). Every one of the Ten Commandments is made an idol, if selfishly interpreted, and not in the spirit and truth of God (John 4 : 23), of obedience, brotherly kindness, and charity. In short all idolatry is selfishness, and all selfishness idolatry—a yielding to the temptations of the world, the flesh, and the devil (Matt. 4 : 1–11).

Again what we call patriotism, devotion to one's country, may be and no doubt largely is idolatrous,—always is, in fact, if it be selfish and exclusive. For only so far as fatherhood in our native land is Fatherhood in God,—that is, only so far as our Government recognizes

the authority of God and exercises such authority,—is it a true Government, and are we
patriotic in our devotion thereto. Otherwise
it is tyranny, and our worship thereof a debasing idolatry, the sundering of our natural and
religious bond of union with God, and the
separating of ourselves from the source whence
we derive all personal and social rights and
liberties. To obey voluntarily, therefore, a
civil ruler who, though superior in power to
ourselves, is himself disobedient to God, or to
voluntarily submit to social laws and conditions
that are in conflict with the consciousness, and
will of God, is the worship of false gods.
Willingly to acquiesce in social evils, to consent to be wronged or to wrong others, renders
us personally responsible therefor. Yet in our
resistance thereto we may not ourselves violate
the supreme conscience and will. We may be
compelled to suffer for a time, but we may
never willingly submit to usurpation,—and all
government is usurpation that is not derived
from and administered in harmony with the
laws of God. As the tares may be permitted
to grow with the wheat until the harvest, lest
in rooting them up the good wheat be destroyed (Matt. 13: 29), so unjust laws may
not be abrogated by violence, if those which

are just are to perish with them, and anarchy result.

The Third Article, forbidding the name of God to be used in vain, affirms that we may neither assume an authority as from God which he has not conferred, nor, if conferred, use it wantonly or oppressively. All rightful authority is derived from a superior power, and ultimately from the one supreme and therefore absolute power of God, and must be exercised in conformity with his conscience and will for the protection and promotion of social rights and interests. If, therefore, one have authority from God to rule others, as the parent the child, he will use it in vain if he does not use it for the good of those he governs. This principle applies to the proper adjustment of all social relations. Each social position, privilege, or possession any individual enjoys must be used for the good of others equally as for his own; for otherwise—if there be not community, and any person selfishly assert exclusive rights in any good gifts of God—whatever he possesses becomes an instrument of oppression, is used selfishly or capriciously, is a vain assumption of rights, and is blasphemy against God. Thus if one person or combination of persons be possessed of great wealth, and claims that because God gave him power to acquire it, he has a right to use it for his own exclusive benefit, and oppresses the poor, this is taking God's name in vain. The same is true of one who, though poor in purse, is strong in mind or body, and—especially if possessed of education and skill—monopolizes and devotes these gifts to his own exclusive benefit. If one simply uses the name of God to emphasize or establish what is foolish as wise, or false as true, he is guilty of blasphemy. And this is especially true of a perverted religious faith, which dogmatically and arbitrarily asserts and enforces as a truth of God that which is either false, uncertain, or not essential to our salvation —thereby limiting the opportunities and possibilities of social redemption. And finally if one uses the moral law, or any other law, to disguise his own inconsistencies or hypocrisies, saying, "thou shalt not steal," when he himself is a thief; or "thou shalt not commit adultery," when he himself is an adulterer; or makes his boast in the law which he himself transgresses, he dishonors the name of God (Rom. 2: 21-23).

The Fourth Article affirms the duty, necessity, and opportunity of devoting one day in seven to rest and the culture of holiness. Not, however, that there need or should be only one

day in seven of rest and holiness, for in a perfect social state all days are restful and holy,
but that such rest and holiness are the natural
evolution of good works and right religious
culture, and represent social conditions in harmony with the consciousness and will of God.
This is evident from the concluding words of
this article—"*for* in six days the Lord made
heaven and earth, the sea and all that in them
is, and rested the seventh day; *wherefore* the
Lord blessed the seventh day and hallowed it."
As the seventh period in the cycle of the
world's evolution from chaos for the abode of
Man represented a complete and perfect work,
so every seventh day in the process of man's
social redemption from sin is made in this
article of the moral law a perpetual symbol, re-
membrance, prophecy, and promise of its ultimate completion and realization. What our
true social ideal should be—the mark set before
us—is an ultimate condition of rest and holiness; and the true and practical observance of
the sabbath—so far as our oppressed condition
will permit—is in our efforts to realize such
ideal.

So far and so long as we can and do re-
member the sabbath day and keep it holy, there
is a reasonable hope of our ultimate and com-

plete redemption,—hope that we may finally be redeemed from the otherwise perpetual toil and bondage to which we are subjected. If for one day in seven we may rest, it is plainly possible for us to rest every day. If for one day we may be holy—that is pure in spirit and in truth—so may we ever be undefiled by selfishness and sin. The true idea of rest is not cessation from all activities and works—though in our corrupt social condition, in which we are subjected to constant and excessive toil, it is thus interpreted and limited—but relief from such enforced and oppressive labors as repress and limit freedom, life, and enjoyment—such rest as the slave naturally feels when emancipated from the thralldom of debasing and cruel servitude. So also the true idea of holiness is not austerity, but cheerfulness and health of mind and body, purity and spirituality, sensibility of grace and gratitude toward God, and of brotherly kindness.

Such rest and holiness we may feel and cultivate in God's appointed sabbaths; and the more we realize their influence in our everyday life, the freer and happier will our social conditions become, until all selfishness and oppression cease, and our life becomes a continual sabbath.

Our nature is both animal and spiritual, and it is essential to our well-being that these two elements should be harmonious and rightly balanced, as in God are his nature and art. Man does not live by bread alone, but by every word that proceedeth out of the mouth of God (Matt. 4: 4), and hence may not devote his time and labors unduly to the promotion of material interests (Rom. 8: 6). The law that correlates natural forces maintains harmony also in those which are spiritual—these two being correlatives, not differing from each other at all in principles (Eph. 2: 21, 22)—what is law in one world being also law in every other world. Essential, therefore, as are our secular interests, our spiritual interests may not lawfully be sacrificed thereto; and if either voluntarily or by compulsion we devote ourselves wholly or chiefly to the procurement of our daily bread— especially if we seek to accumulate more than is essential to our healthful necessities—we are brutalized thereby.

By bread we mean all things that nourish and strengthen our animal nature, although there is a bread which in like manner nourishes and strengthens our spiritual being, and which comes, not from the earth, but down from heaven (John 6: 32, 34).   Money, food, dress,

and shelter, and all other things developed
from the earth, or constructed by our hands,
are bread so far as they contribute to our comfort and well-being in this world, and are real
riches ; but like the manna by which the children of Israel were fed in the wilderness, they
corrupt if we accumulate and hoard them
beyond what our immediate necessities require.
As the love of money is a root of all evil
(1 Tim. 6: 10), so the love of bread which
money procures—all earthly riches—has become
a great and terrible dissipation, and the root of
well-nigh all social evils. We call its culture
business, and have become so devoted thereto
that we regard it as our chiefest virtue—so devoted that we bow down to it and worship it as
our god, make it the chief end and aim of life,
that for which we live and die—no person being
popularly considered " well off " while he lives
or when he dies, unless he has accumulated and
hoarded more than is essential to his daily
needs. Having thus yielded ourselves body
and soul to the first temptation of Satan—to
converting stones to bread—we have thereby
become utterly enslaved to him, and he has re-
warded us by converting us into a society of
moths, rusts, and thieves, afflicted us with a
legion of devils that breed innumerable and

tormenting social diseases and conditions of suffering. While industrial activity is no doubt a necessity to sinful men—our sins having caused the earth, from which we derive our physical life, as a natural sequence of our transgression of natural laws to bring forth thorns and thistles, having cursed the earth for our sake, and compelled us to eat our bread in the sweat of our faces—there is yet no glory in simply toiling to live, or in living to toil. Excessive labor only serves to aggravate and increase the curse imposed upon us for our transgressions; and for this reason are we commanded to refrain wholly therefrom one day in seven. Yet like every other law, if it be obeyed only in the letter and not in the spirit, (2 Cor. 3 : 6), it may be practically annulled by its observance, and even perverted to evil purposes. Thus it may be observed with such austerity as to become burdensome and oppressive, and not a day of cheerfulness and relaxation ; or with such excess of license and self-indulgence as to render it an occasion for dissipation and riotous living. As the sabbath was made for man and not man for the sabbath (Mark 2 : 27)—that is, for his use and not his abuse, for his freedom and not his enslavement, —anything that promotes his best interests is its proper observance, and anything prejudicial thereto is in violation of its spirit. It is the ideal of the heavenly rest—a social condition in which, when attained, though it be one of unbounded freedom and activity, there are no compulsory and enslaving labors (Rev. 14: 13).

But if, as we have affirmed, the spirit of the sabbath should enter into our everyday life, we may violate this law every other day in the week as well as on the seventh. That is, the spirit of unrest and unholiness may, by excessive devotion to business, so enter into our life as to wholly neutralize the spirit of the sabbath. In fact, society may and does devote itself so excessively to business that it avails itself of the sabbath for the most part only as a means of continuing such excess—using its rest, as it uses sleep, for the purpose only of recuperating its exhausted animal life, that it may indulge the more in its business dissipations. This is plainly the perversion and violation of this law—preventing true rest and holiness becoming the fruits of its labors. As like naturally produces like, unnatural devotion to business cannot produce natural rest, unholiness holiness, nor social enslavement social freedom. Hence, if we would approximate

that perfect social condition of rest and holiness foreshadowed, prophesied, and promised
in God's sabbath, we must limit our labors
more and more, until there is no excess thereof
beyond what our actual necessities require.
Doubtless even now, sinful as the world is, a
few hours of daily labor would be quite sufficient to supply our physical comforts. Any
more than this, therefore, is dissipation; and
any person who voluntarily, from motives of
avarice and cupidity, devotes himself to business more than is essential to the procurement
of his daily bread—or any person who requires
others dependent upon him for work or livelihood to do this—is a sabbath-breaker, and is
also guilty of the transgression of every other
moral law—even though he observe it strictly
in the letter (Jas. 2: 10).

The Fifth Article affirms the social duty of children to honor and obey their parents. Whatever
in a true sense is social is in a like sense just,
rational, and moral, and is derived from the
Supreme Authority. The authority of the parent over the child, being derived directly from
God who is our common Father, is a natural
and just authority. As parents are themselves
children, and as children become parents, all
society is honored if children honor their par-

ents; and on the other hand is dishonored if
this commandment is broken.

By honoring parents is meant obeying and
loving them—responsiveness to their grace and
loving kindness toward us, and living such a
life as shall best contribute to their welfare,
glory and happiness in us. But as the parent's
authority is derived wholly from God, it must
be exercised in a just, rational, and moral way,
or it will become tyrannical and cruel. It
must be in harmony with the consciousness and
will of God, and exerted for the well-being of
the child and the best interests of society.
Otherwise he forfeits his authority, and should
not be permitted to control the child. He cannot lawfully be capricious or selfish, for in such
case he dishonors God, society, and his children, and is not entitled to honor. Moreover,
since the infirmities of the parent are, by the
natural evolution of like from like, transmitted
to the child—else what is good in the parent
could not be transmitted to the child—no person has a right, or should be permitted, to become a parent if he be unfitted either in body
or mind to produce reasonably healthy offspring—such as are equal or superior to the
average child in this respect. In other words,
if an unnatural parent is justly deprived of his

natural right to the control of his child, so also is every person of vitiated nature justly deprived of his natural right to become a parent. And as it is manifestly impossible for children to honor dishonorable parents—especially when they are themselves made dishonorable by their parents—and society is composed wholly of parents and children, it is absolutely essential to the observance of this commandment, and of primary importance in the promotion of our social well-being, that parentage should be improved—which is only possible by the improvement of public morality.

While therefore this fifth commandment is addressed to children, it is operative only to the degree that their parents are moral men and women; and as children become parents, they can only honor their parents by becoming themselves moral men and women. But morality must be such in the spirit as well as in the letter. Hence, though one does not break the letter of the law, yet if his influence in society is such as to constrain or permit others to do so, he is a transgressor. One may even— and this is by no means uncommon—outwardly seek to promote morality in the community, yet be guilty through his own selfishness, whereby many are reduced to poverty and doomed to

excessive and brutalizing toil, of dishonoring
his parents by rendering honorable parentage
in others impossible ; and as his selfishness renders him immoral in spirit, and subjects him to
just punishment, he cannot himself become an
honorable parent or produce healthy offspring.
But while excess of toil is unnatural and immoral, it is not more unnatural and immoral
than the idleness, luxury, and extravagance
which produce excessive toil—every man being
himself a brute who brutalizes others.

The Sixth Article affirms the natural right
of every person who has not consciously and
wilfully forfeited this right, to the full possession and enjoyment of natural life.   And this
includes all social privileges and means by
which life is developed and cultured, as also all
its varieties, whether physical, mental or spiritual.   Life is limitless in God, and is transmitted to all men in the full measure of their
capacities to receive and enjoy.   Every organ
of the body, as also every faculty of the mind,
is its natural receptacle and organ of trans-
mission, and to destroy these is to cut life off
from this world, and to defeat God's purposes
in our creation and existence here.   Moreover,
as life is the medium of all activity, joy, and
beauty,—of every perception, emotion, or vo-

lition—its destruction is the complete obliteration here of all social rights and possessions natural or acquired. To this law there are no exceptions or qualifications—understanding, of course, that it is applied only for the protection of those who obey, every transgression naturally limiting and decreasing our capacity to receive or retain life.

" Thou shalt not kill " prohibits all destruction of innocent life, though one life may be sacrificed for a better life, in which case it is not destroyed but exchanged, whether by an individual or society—understanding by innocent life one that is not itself guilty of killing, either directly by violence, or indirectly by a slow process of repression ; by malice, passion, indifference, neglect or needless ignorance. Nor is killing limited to complete destruction. Any repression of life that prevents the free exercise and development of our faculties of body or mind, either by imposing thereon unnatural burdens, or by hindering or neglecting their proper nourishment and culture, whereby the increase and health they might otherwise attain are not realized, is violation of this law. In short this law not only requires society to pro-tect its life from destruction by actual violence, but also from all evil influences that impair its

healthful activities—from unhealthful surroundings and unnatural conditions and habits
of living; from oppressive systems whereby it
is dwarfed and brutalized; from all dissipations and excesses; and from the malignant
spirits of pride, envy, cupidity and selfishness.

The Seventh Article requires fidelity, purity,
and stability in the relations of husband and
wife. Adultery is the general term used in the
bible to define all acts or impulses that tend to
the vitiation of right social relations as ordained in the natural and moral laws of God,
and which constitute true religion. Hence irreligion is adulterous (Jer. 3: 8, 9; Ezek.
23: 37; Matt. 12: 39; 2 Pet. 2: 14); and as
marriage is a primary social institution ordained of God, whereby human life is not only
evolved and perpetuated, but also its character
mainly determined, this article is introduced
into the moral code, affirming its sacredness,
and prohibiting unfaithfulness to its obligations. As by natural law like produces like,
as are the parents so are the children in their
constitutions and dispositions both of body and
mind; and though children after birth, may
be improved by art, yet as the foundation of
their culture thus acquired must be their
natural strength and character, the degree of

their possible improvement must be determined thereby. That is, the degree of culture to which children may attain is limited by the degree of physical and mental power they inherit from their parents; and as all members of society are children, and the offspring of marriage, anything whatever that tends to impair its purity and stability or vitiate its character, is in the highest degree detrimental to social interests.

But adultery does not consist simply in infidelity to the marriage bonds as established by civil laws, but also in marriage itself when the parties thereto are united from any other motive or principle thereof than true religion, which is the theory and practice of love. Hence, if its motive is merely sensual, mercenary, heedless of natural and moral law, or indifferent to parental obligations incurred thereby, it is unlawful. Adultery consists also in depraved social conditions which impel thereto, so that society itself, though it legalizes marriage and punishes transgression of the letter of the law, is itself adulterous by permitting such conditions to exist. Cupidity, luxury, and extravagance, and the corresponding conditions of thriftlessness, squalor, and indigency, not only tend to limit marriages among all classes, but also to so disqualify the sexes therefor as to render them, when contracted, vicious and unstable. The present instability is not, as many suppose, mainly the result of laxity in the civil laws whereby marriage is permitted or annulled, but is symptomatic of our vitiated social culture and condition, and can only be remedied by the practical application of the principles of true religion to the right adjustment of social relations.

The Eighth Article, prohibiting theft, affirms the right of all men to the possession, control, and enjoyment of their possessions naturally and lawfully acquired. Other things being equal, the natural possessions of all individuals —those acquired of God, and those naturally transmitted from parents to children—are equal. But as a matter of fact in a sinful world other things are not equal, some persons being more experienced, intelligent, enterprising, or economical than others ; and it should be manifestly unnatural—nay, absolutely impossible—that some should not possess more than others.

Men are not born equal in capacities or opportunities, nor are they equally disposed to improve their capacities and opportunities for increase ; and while this fact does not permit

any person selfishly to possess his own, it renders the absolutely equal distribution of personal wealth impossible.   Nor is such distribution to be desired.   As individuality cannot
be exclusive of sociality, neither can individual
possessions be exclusive of social interests.
The wealth of society is the aggregate possessions of the individuals that compose it; and
as by society all persons are made one, there
is practically in a right condition of society a
social equality of possessions, the poor sharing
equally with the rich according to their ability
to receive and use for the common good of
all.   Hence, if society be rightly constituted,
no wrong or oppression can arise from personal inequalities in the possessions of individual members.   What society should be is a
moral condition in which there is no theft—in
which the theory of mutual love, which is
true religion, is applied and practiced—of
mutual participation in our natural and justly
acquired rights, of mutual help, and the unlimited freedom of each member in the increase of
his possessions and capacities for enjoyment.

Man, therefore, being a social being, his right
to possess, while otherwise limitless is not exclusive—not the right of one to use and enjoy
the wealth he controls to his own exclusive

use, but also for the use of others as well as of
himself. In fact, to the degree we make our
right to possess individual and exclusive it
ceases to be right, and becomes a trespass upon
the rights of others. " Thou shalt not steal,"
means not only that one shall not rob another
of his property, but also that he shall not limit
another's opportunity and right to acquire
property. That is, it is equally theft for one
citizen to prevent his fellow-citizen from acquiring riches, as it is to deprive him of that
he has already acquired. To the degree only
that I feel that what is mine is also yours according to my ability to bestow, and yours to
receive, am I a moral man. The moral code
we are considering was made for the protection
of all men in their natural rights, and not by
its perversion to give impunity in the indulgence of selfishness and avarice. The natural
power to acquire riches is unlimited, whether
of objective possessions or of subjective capacities of enjoying them ; and in no case is it
essential to their possession, enjoyment, and increase that one member or class of society
should be kept poor that another may be rich.
In fact we are rich only to the degree we can
and do make others rich as well as ourselves.
Thus if one be strong physically or mentally, it

is not necessary to the enjoyment of his
strength that others should be kept weak—that
he should enslave them and make their strength
tributary to his own—to compel them to toil
for his support in idleness, luxury, or dissipation. It is sufficient that he has the greater
power to help himself and others; and if we
were unselfish, the richer we are the richer also
would others be. Nay, it is impossible for us
to be rich at all, except we be rich toward God
and each other (Luke 12: 15–21); for no person can otherwise save his riches any more
than he can his own soul (Matt. 16: 26). Every
selfish person is, to the degree of his selfishness, a thief and an enemy of society, and in
rebellion against God.

But as the rich man who oppresses the poor
is a thief, so also is the poor man who by lack
of enterprise and thrift fails to improve his
natural gifts in the acquirement of riches, or
by dissipation wastes and squanders them—
thus making himself an unnecessary burden
upon the charities of society. So also is any
man a thief, whether rich or poor, who is uncharitable, unjust, or dishonest—does not give
as he receives; pays his employee less than he
can afford to give, or charges his employer more
than his just wages; sells his merchandise for

more than it is worth, or buys for less. In short, all riches must be accumulated and developed by the exercise and use of our natural gifts of God, and in accordance with the letter and spirit of his moral laws, or their possession is unlawful.

The Ninth Article prohibits our bearing false witness against our neighbor. Truth is the harmonious relation of substance, nature, and art to each other, and truthfulness the expression of such harmonious relation. And as Substance, Nature, and Art in God are eternal and invariable, so also is the Truth in him, and all expressions thereof. So far, therefore, as we are, in the elements of our being, in harmony with God are we true, and in all we are, do, or feel we bear witness to the truth; but otherwise,—so far as our conditions, individually or socially, are inharmonious—are we false witnesses.

Lack of truth is lack of principle; and lack of principle is lack of completeness and harmony in such elements of our being as are essential to our well-being—to health, life, freedom, joy, beauty. All untruthfulness, whether of words spoken or unspoken, of deeds done or omitted to be done, of relations or conditions personal or social, of emotions of sympathy or desire felt or unfelt, of pride or envy, of letter or spirit, is dishonest and bearing false witness against our neighbors; for as we are social beings we cannot exist without being examples to each other, and just so far as our examples are false are we unsocial, irreligious, and trespassers upon each other's rights. In short, anything in us renders us liars that impairs mutual faith and trust—any dishonesty, insincerity, infidelity, unkindness, selfish pride, envy, or cupidity.

The Tenth Article forbids us to covet anything that is our neighbor's. Not that it is wrong to covet, for a covetous motive is innate in our nature, and inspires all true aspirations and efforts for increase in possessions and enjoyments—and we are exhorted to covet earnestly the best gifts (1 Cor. 12: 31)—but that we may not desire to deprive others of any things that are theirs.

Interpreted also in the spirit, this article prohibits us not only from desiring to deprive others of what is lawfully theirs, but also from seeking to prevent their possessing such things as they may lawfully acquire. Thus, if I am poor, and my neighbor rich, and I would deprive him of his riches, I am a transgressor of this law; or if I am rich, and he poor, I am equally a transgressor if I would deprive him of his just right and opportunity of becoming rich. Being mutually and naturally dependent and helpful, we cannot rightfully do or desire to do unto others anything we would not they should do unto us. And while there is no limit placed upon the just accumulation of riches, all increase is unlawful which is acquired through the impoverishment of others.

Covetousness is in the motive or spirit, not in act or letter. But when perverted to selfishness, it inspires and becomes in itself the transgression of every moral law. To covet and to love are of like meaning, differing only as the true spirit of the law differs from that of the gospel, love being the fulfillment of the law. Hence, as love is the crowning virtue, and without love there is no virtue, so this Tenth Article of the moral law defines the crowning principle of morality, without which there is no morality. In other words, without the spirit of unselfish aspirations and desires, all morality is but as sounding brass and a tinkling cymbal.

Wherefore, both in the Old and New Testaments, we find selfish covetousness interpreted as the sum of all vices—the natural spirit of sociality and religion perverted, not only into the spirit of indifference to the welfare of others, but also of cruelty and oppression—the root of all avarice and lust, of idolatry and adultery, of envy and pride, of murder and theft, of bigotry and self-righteousness, of blasphemy, lying, and hypocrisy, of disobedience and rebellion, of slothfulness, extravagance, and dissipation; in short, of every vicious love, of which is developed vice and crime (Ps. 10: 2, 3; Mic. 2: 2; Hab. 2: 9, 11; Luke 12: 15-20; 16: 14, 15; Rom. 7: 7, 8; 2 Pet. 2: 3).

Such in brief is the moral law, whereby, in the disciplinary stage of human culture, are defined and enforced our just social obligations and rights, which though perverted to vain and selfish uses by the people with whom it originated, is absolutely essential to true religion, and a just community of social interests.

PART III.

THE SOCIALISTIC IDEA OF THE CHURCH.

ALTHOUGH the law of man's natural intuitions of social obligations and rights, evolved and developed by Divine Art, accurately and fully defines such obligations and rights, it does not represent the highest culture of religion. As in the training of our childhood until it reaches the age of discretion, so also in the primary culture of the human race, was it necessary that it should be subjected to discipline until it was able to distinguish between right and wrong, and to choose what was good and reject what was evil (Gen. 2: 16, 17; Deut. 30: 15, 19). And necessarily such discipline must be by instruction in the principles of true religion, and by the practical applications of such principles in the enforcement of social laws founded thereon—religion being our unity with God as our common Father, and with each other as brethren. But as such unity must exist in the spirit as well as in the letter—in love as well as in law—it is plain that the highest culture

84

of religion cannot be attained by enforced obedience to God, and enforced respect to each other's rights, but by voluntary obedience and respect—realized only in unselfish love of our Father and our brother men. That is, unity is complete only when law is fulfilled in love (Rom. 13 : 10)—by choice rather than by compulsion; for otherwise—so long as the law is fulfilled by compulsion—there is fear, and fear is bondage (Rom. 8: 15; Heb. 2: 15); and as in true religion there is perfect freedom (John 8: 32; Rom. 8: 21), it cannot be fully realized in enforced obedience to the moral law. "But perfect love casteth out fear."

Now as the theory and practice of the moral law were represented in the Temple, so are the theory and practice of love represented in the Church, in the extension and development of which Peter and John were pioneers. They were among the immediate converts and disciples of Jesus the Christ, the original founder of the Church, and, in advance of the religious culture of their day, were endeavoring to put in practice his social theory, whereby they believed all oppression would be put away, and all men dwell together in the love of God and in peace and good will toward each other. Like all other true theories, this had previously

existed only in ideal conceptions evolved of
human longings and aspirations, inspired, as all
such longings and aspirations must naturally
be, of the Spirit of God, the source of all pure
idealisms,—in dreams, whisperings, and prophecies of better things to come; and finally, it
is believed, practically realized in our social
life by an example of perfected human nature
and art, a God-Man who represented in person
the express image of the Father, (Heb. 1: 3)
—which, if true, is conclusive evidence that a
like perfection of nature and art is a possibility
of attainment by every member of the human
family.

This example, therefore, of a perfected human nature and art was, as are all new creations
and improvements, a natural evolution of preceding and accompanying social conditions,
since whatever is is necessarily the outcome and
continuity of what has been before, although
nature—which simply perpetuates itself—may
be so improved by art that out of imperfection
and corruption may come forth perfection and
incorruption (1 Cor. 13: 9-12; 15: 53).

"When the fullness of time had come"
(Gal. 4: 4, 5; Eph. 1: 10)—that is, when it became possible by previous religious culture to
realize practically the prophetic social idea of

sonship and brotherhood in God, and its "glorious liberty"—there was evolved a human
being in such perfect unity in substance, nature
and art with the Divine, that he was justly regarded by his followers, and practically was,
both God and man (John 10: 30)—calling
himself the Son of God, and the Son of Man;
so that as God is in Substance, Nature, and Art,
he was the Word, that is, the expression, in
human substance, nature, and art (John 1: 1);
and of what is the Divine conception of social
order, he was the example and teacher. He
announced his social polity to be that of the
Kingdom of God (Mark 4: 11)—a gospel of
glad tidings of great joy (Luke 1: 19; 8: 1),
and its practical development in the world to
be his Church, Congregation, or School, representing in its organic unity and works the theory
and practice of love (John 13: 34), whose ultimate design was to embrace all human beings
in one Fold, or Family (John 10: 16; Eph. 3:
15). It differs from the Temple only as love
differs from law, it being the fulfillment of the
law in love—the practical realization of the
ultimate purpose of the law of charity in the
fruition of faith and hope (Rom. 13: 9, 10).
Both are of God and alike socialistic in spirit;
but while one is only a partial development of

religion, the other is the perfection and fullness thereof.

Now if it be true that God Is, there must also be a Kingdom of God—a community in which law is fulfilled in love, and in which there are perfect liberty, equality, and fraternity in harmony with the divine consciousness and will; for necessarily Being must be limitless in its comprehensions of social conditions as in all things else. Hence we may define Christianity as an effort to introduce into this sinful world the social system of that Kingdom. And this effort, corrupt and selfish as this world is, cannot be impossible of realization, for the citizens of that Kingdom, being creatures of God, must be of our social nature, and can differ from us only in their superior culture in the principles of true religion. Moreover, the first step thereto, as in the creation of man in this world there must have been produced a first man, of the earth, earthy, was necessarily the development from that earth-man of a second man (1 Cor. 15 : 45, 47), of heaven, heavenly, conceived in the spirit of the earth-man from the Spirit of God:—that is, an ideal conception of an improved and higher order of manhood imparted to the mind of the earth-man from the Divine Consciousness,—which is

nothing more than to say that, as the infant
which possesses little consciousness grows into
the consciousness of manhood, so the human
race in mind and spirit has grown into the consciousness of revealed religious truths.   In fact,
the infant *is* naturally the earth-man, and its
true and perfected manhood is the Lord from
heaven.

The beginning and process, therefore, of the
development in the flesh of the God-man, "the
Lord from heaven," were not, as nothing enduring can be, contrary to nature, howbeit he
existed from eternity in spirit as the primary
and personal realization of Sonship, the first
begotten of the Father—"was in the beginning
with God and was God,"—but was naturally
and prophetically conceived of in the human
conscience of the Consciousness of God—that
is, begotten in the spirit of man of the Spirit of
God, thereby inspiring aspirations and hopes of
realizing this Divine Sonship in our earthy life.
In other words, as all heavenly aspirations,
hopes, and prophecies naturally realize themselves in our outward life, there was naturally
produced in the flesh a human being of perfected nature and art expressive of the Divine—
one who, when grown to manhood, became the
express image in human personality of the

Divine Personality (John 14: 9; 2 Cor. 4: 4; Col. 1: 15; Heb. 1: 13).

But whatever be true theoretically of the evolution of Jesus the Christ in human society, it cannot be questioned that he was, so far as we are able to conceive thereof, a perfect man, the incarnation of a divine manhood and sonship, or that his existence here in human society is the conclusive evidence that a like perfection is a possible development of improved human nature and art.

Conceding, therefore, that his birth was not miraculous in an unnatural sense, but a natural evolution of the religious culture of his family whereby the law was fulfilled in love, the fact still remains that, as human nature became perfected in him, so may it also in the whole human race. That such a human being existed here is certain, as evidenced by the existence of his gospel and church, in which are fully and clearly defined and illustrated the principles of true religion—a social polity which, if practically applied and realized would redeem society from all sin, selfishness, and oppression, and develop a kingdom of God on earth, a state of perfect liberty, equality, and fraternity. What this one man was all may become—sons and prophets of God (Rom. 8: 14; 1 John 3: 1, 12), inspired, begotten in spirit of his ideal of a perfected human nature and art to a new and immortal life —quickened in spirit by the resurrective power of Divine Love (1 Pet. 3: 18).

Every true prophet is one who not only discerns that which may and ought to be, but who also seeks to practically realize his prophetic ideals in himself and in the world,—not only an idealist, but also one who strives to make real that of which at first he only dreams. In the confidence of his inspirations—which, so far from being unnatural, are the natural evolutions of his unity with God in conscience and volition, he is able to receive of his Spirit heavenly ideals—immaculate conceptions in his own spirit of the Spirit of God, which in due time are incarnated, born of the flesh, and made visible in practical life.

As a man is in nature a social being, true prophecy is naturally socialistic; and although it is difficult to trace its source in the obscurity of the remote past in which this prophecy of the coming of a perfected humanity originated, it is clear that it has had a natural, that is a rational, development—as natural in the spirit as the conception, growth and birth of a natural body in the flesh, the development of body and mind being coincident.

God has always had his witnesses (Isa. 43:
9, 10; Heb. 12: 1)—examples of men in this
world conceived in spirit of his Spirit, yet
born naturally of woman in the flesh, whereby
a perfected humanity was approximated by the
Divine Art. Such witnesses were the true
prophets and priests of God, who, though
widely separated in time and space, were yet
bound together in a common faith and trust in
one only living and true God, and constituted
that mystic brotherhood known as the Order
of Melchizedek (Gen. 14: 18). From and by
this Order were evolved and developed the
prophecy of a coming Messiah (Ps. 110: 4;
Heb. 5: 6-10), and the idea of a perfected
social condition of peace and brotherhood (Isa.
11: 1-10; Heb. 7: 1, 2). In its Sonship in
the Father, and in its unity and Brotherhood
in Man, like the Church which is the forebirth
of the Kingdom of God, this divine Order was
counted as eternal in God, " having neither beginning of days nor end of life," being " made,
not after the law of a carnal commandment,
but after the power of an endless life " (Heb.
7: 3, 16)—the idea of the finite and temporal
being merged in and swallowed up of the Infinite and Eternal (2 Cor. 5: 4)—even as in-

fancy is merged in and swallowed up of manhood (1 Cor. 13: 11, 12).

This prophecy, however, of a perfected humanity found at first but feeble expression—in covenants and promises (Gen. 3: 15; 9: 13, 14; 17: 7)—in whisperings, dreams, visions, and foreshadowings of a glory to come (Gen. 15: 1, 17; 28: 12; Ex. 3: 2). But when these ideal conceptions had been partially realized in the development of a theocracy under the Moral Law, the prophets of this Divine Order—sensible of the severe yet necessary discipline and thralldom imposed thereby, and inspired of God with a higher conception of social freedom, while at the same time they became the more conscious of their own imperfection and weakness—began to prophesy of the coming of One whom, in the perfection of human nature and art they described as the Redeemer (Job 19: 25; Isa. 59: 20), God with man (Isa. 7: 14; 9: 6), The Wonderful, The Counsellor, The Mighty God, The Everlasting Father, The Prince of Peace. And striving further in the rapture of their contemplations to portray in words this ideal Manhood, they defined his mission to be, "To bind up the broken-hearted, to proclaim liberty to the captives, and the opening of the prison to them that are bound " (Isa. 61: 1).

Fragmentary and confused as these prophecies may appear, they became coherent and definite in the example of a perfected humanity in Jesus the Christ. Hence Peter and John believed they had been historically and spiritually fulfilled in him—that he was the promised Redeemer, Prince of Peace, and God with Man. And it must be conceded that in nature and art, judged by his teachings and works, he could not have been other than the full expression in the human conscience and will of the Divine Consciousness and Will. And whether it be literally or figuratively true that at his birth was heard the Angelic Chant, it is certain that his coming was in fact the proclamation of "Glory to God in the highest, and on earth peace, good will toward men "—expressive of a social and religious unity of God and Man, which, if practically realized, would bind up the broken-hearted, and open every prison door.

It is indeed self-evident that, if the religious bond of which we have spoken were practically realized—if men would love God with all their heart, mind, and soul, and their neighbors as themselves—all natural and lawfully acquired rights would be gladly recognized. And it is equally certain that such rights cannot in any other way be secured; for just so long as men are selfish will they trespass upon them, and the strong oppress the weak.

Now Peter and John represented this higher religious culture, the principles of which were as fully and accurately defined and classified by the Christ and his Apostles as were those of the moral law by Moses and the prophets; and as love is the fulfilling of the law, such principles are represented in the methods by which law is fulfilled in love. Thus the first commandment of the law, which affirms the existence of one only living and true God, and requires us to recognize in him the supreme and ultimate Source of all authority, is, so far as appears from the letter thereof, simply the promulgation of a decree as arbitrary and despotic as that of any earthly sovereign, who, on the false assumption that "might makes right," exercises his authority simply because he has power to enforce it—even as Nebuchadnezzar required all his subjects to fall down and worship the golden image which he had set up. But interpreted and fulfilled in the spirit, whereby the true idea of God is made to appear that of a universal Father, ruling in love, and for the best interests of all his children, all ideas of caprice and tyranny in him may be banished from our minds, and the humility of our worship become the medium of our highest exaltation (Matt. 18: 4). This, therefore, is the first and cardinal principle affirmed and taught in the gospel of the Christ—the universal Fatherhood of God; and that in such Fatherhood only is the supreme Source of all rightful authority and power. Of this, and of this only, is derived the right idea of one only living and true God; for otherwise, if our interests, our very being and life, were not identified with his, as those of children with parents in one family, it is impossible that there should be unity of men with God; and without unity there could be no true religion. If he were a being separate and apart from us, unlike us in nature and art, his authority would be derived simply from his superior power, and it would be impossible that what were his private interests should be also ours. In fact, if he were not our Father, if we were not begotten of him, —he might be totally unlike us; and as we are possessed of rational and moral faculties, he might be without reason or conscience, and our devotion to him be only idolatry, an unnatural subjection to a being inferior to ourselves. His superiority must be in the same qualities

of mind and heart that we ourselves possess—
the full perfection of our reason and conscience
—or he could not be our supreme authority in
reason and conscience, nor could he love us or
we him.   But if, as taught in the gospel of the
Christ, we are his children, then is the human
race his natural family, true religion our unity
with him and each other, and our worship the
culture of obedience to a living and loving
Father.

If then we understand what the true idea of
Fatherhood is—of One who has begotten us to
life of his own Life, endowed us with personality of his own Personality, and protects and
governs us in our own best interests—we have
the right idea of God, and can understand how
all his laws are fulfilled in love,—his relations
to us being precisely the same as those of a true
unselfish earthly father to his children, in which
there is no caprice or tyranny.

Now this idea of God as the universal Father
represents the cardinal principle of the Christian religion, even as that of one only living
and true God represents the cardinal principle
of the moral law.   With this idea, and this
only, is it possible to rightly interpret the
spirit of the law, or fulfill it in love.   With
this idea and this only, practically applied, is it

possible for any man to become a true follower
of the Christ. " Our Father " being the postulate of what is known as the Lord's Prayer, all
its hopes and aspirations, as are also all the
teachings of his gospel, are founded thereon,
and all its promises realized therein.

Is this postulate true? Is the Supreme
Power and Intelligence that is certainly manifested in all things that exist our Universal
Father? Or is this idea merely fanciful and
sentimental, or based only on the assertion
of Scripture that God made, brought forth,
created, or caused to grow, man in his likeness,
both male and female (Gen. 1: 26, 27)?—or
upon the declaration of the Christ that he himself came forth from the Father (John 16: 28)?
No doubt it is both scripturally and logically
true; for the supreme Power and Intelligence
—recognized and defined even by unchristian
men as the " Unknown God " (Acts 17: 23)—
must be the Person, the Original Man, from
whom all persons are derived, and in whom we
live and move and have our being (Acts 17:
28); or, as accurately and authoritatively defined in Scripture, the "I Am That I AM"
(Ex. 3: 14)—the Infinite, Absolute and sole
Reality of Personal Being, of Whom all finite
beings are realizations, births, or natural evolu-

tions, even as substantives are realizations of Substance.

Moreover, as is asserted and logically demonstrated in the apostolic writings, and especially in those of Paul and John, God is our loving Father,—nay Love Itself (John 4: 8). Indeed, it is a truth as positively demonstrable in natural as in spiritual science, that all things visible and invisible in the entire Universe are of love, by love, and for love. That is, all persons or things, all lives, lights, thoughts, and emotions, are begotten, born, made to appear, created, whether of substance, nature, or art, of love—howbeit love, as all things else, may be corrupted by sin. Indeed, every faculty we possess is a faculty of love, a power and passion of creating and enjoying what we create.

Now let us have a practical idea of what love is ; for when Paul declares that love is the fulfilling of the law, and John that God is Love, they do not use the word in a merely sentimental or unphilosophical sense. God being Substance, Nature, and Art, such also is Love, if John's definition be true. That is, these three cardinal elements of Being, united as they are in harmonious relations, are the realizations of Love—the Word or Expression of

Love. They came forth of Love, were in the beginning with love, and are Love. For manifestly they represent and are the eternal unity and harmony of Being. Naturally, however, things do not unite and become one except there be affinity; and such affinity is mutual love. And as no being could be except by union of two or more things, such affinity or love is the ultimate Principle of Being—at least so far as our finite conceptions of Infinite Being can reach. And moreover, if Being be Personal, our primary and practical conception of God is that he is Personal Love—the Unity of all elements of personality comprehended in the titles of Father, Son, and Spirit.

At first thought we may infer that from such unity of Substance, Nature, and Art Personality was evolved, but the contrary is evidently true. Neither Substance, Nature, nor Art could have ever been apart from each other, or from Personality; and as together they represent Being, Being must have evolved them. Hence, as Being is Personal, Person must have evolved them, and they exist only as elements of Personality evolved of Person. As Infinite Being cannot be limited to conditions and relations of time and space, any idea of its origin is manifestly fanciful, and really absurd

—for of course there can be no origin in time
or space of that which is without beginning
or ending—yet we may have a clear conception, from " things which do appear" (Heb.
11: 3), of what that uncreated Being or Person Is.   If it manifests itself in love, of which
we have power of conscience, and love is the
medium by which all things are made to appear and grow, it is evident that love is our
true and primary conception of God—the original, uncreated, and First Cause of all things,
visible and invisible.   And as Love is Unity,
God is the Unity of all things.   This Unity
produces and requires law and order, and is,
therefore, the fulfilling of the law.   Or as John
expresses the same idea, " everyone that loveth
is born of God and knoweth God."   In other
words, right social relations, representing as
they do social harmony and obedience to
Divine laws, precisely and practically expresses
what true love is, and is true religion.

Manifestly, love is the primary realization of
God, not only of himself but of us.   That is,
his self-consciousness is consciousness of Love;
and our consciousness of him is of a Supreme
Person who rules in love.   Moreover, as he
is the Infinite Person, his love must be personal and social—not self-love, as it would be

if there were not comprehended in his Being
both Fatherhood and Sonship. Indeed, the
idea of God would not only be impossible of
realization, but would be really absurd and
contradictory, if our idea of him were limited
to Fatherhood—it being impossible that there
should be a father without a son, or a son
without a father.

Hence, to believe that God is the Infinite
Father is to believe that he is also the Infinite
Son. That is, one in Love—nay One Love—
else Being were not One. This, therefore, is
the second cardinal principle of the gospel of
the Christ, that God is a loving Son,—and is
the assertion of our own sonship in God; that
is, that we are not only fathers but also sons in
God—one through mutual love. With this
idea may we spiritually and practically interpret the Fifth Commandment, which requires
children to honor their parents, for necessarily
there could be no moral or religious obligation
on the part of children to honor and obey
an earthly father, unless the father were himself a son of God, and honored and obeyed his
heavenly Father, the source of all rightful
authority. To be a true son of man is to be a
son in God, and to be a true earthly father is
to be a father in God—one Love—in the same

sense that husband and wife, and husband, wife, and children, are one love.

Now if it be true that Jesus was perfect man, he must have been, as is asserted by the apostolic writers, and as he himself also affirmed, in person the express image and likeness of the Father, so that whosoever looked on him looked on the Father, and was in such perfect love and unity with the Father that he and the Father were one (John 1: 18; 10: 30; 14: 9; Heb. 1: 3). And the same would be true of any other human being who had attained a like perfection—even as this world itself would become one with the Kingdom of God if all evil were eliminated—one through mutual love.

Looking still deeper into the mysteries of our being—led step by step by logical induction and the special inspiration of God—the apostles affirm Jesus to be the First and Only Begotten Son of God (John 1: 14; Heb. 1: 6). In the same sense in which he is in unity with the Father, and the express image of the Father, so also is he in unity with the Son, and the express image of the Son. And as Fatherhood and Sonship must both be comprehended in the one Infinite Person,—one Infinite Love —and have existed in Him from eternity, the

Son is properly defined as the First and Only
Begotten of God. Moreover, as Jesus was
perfect man, he was not simply the image of
the Father and the Son, but also expressed the
personal character and embodiment of eternal
Sonship, and was endowed with the personal
power and individuality of the Eternal Son—
even as one brother of the family in which all
are perfect, possesses all the personal power
and individuality that each other and all possess. Hence Jesus, though a man in the flesh,
was, being perfect, the incarnation, revelation,
expression, or word of the Eternal, the First,
and Only Begotten Son of God. Thus John
describes him as the " Word," which was in the
beginning with God and was God. And what
is more surprising—but what a moment's reflection will convince us is true—he declares
that by him were all things made that were
made; for, as has already been shown, Love
being the first realization of God, and all
things being of love and by love, and the Divine Sonship being the personification of Love,
it follows that by this Word, this Expression
of God, all things were made to appear. And
it is also true, as this great apostle declares,
that "In him was life, and the life was the

light of men "—even as by the natural sun are all natural life and light created.

Hence Jesus properly asserted his Sonship both in man and God, declaring that all things were by the Father delivered into his hands (Matt. 11: 27); and in his teachings, example, and works illustrated what such true sonship is—obedience to the Father, not only because he is superior in power, but because he loves us, and all his laws are established and enforced for our own present and eternal well-being.

The Third cardinal principle is the universal Brotherhood of man (Matt. 23: 8, 9; Mark 3: 31–35; Acts 17: 26; Eph. 4: 25). As all men are sons of God all are members of one Family (Eph. 2: 19; 3: 14, 15). Hence, each is required not only to love God with all his heart, mind, and soul, but also his neighbor as himself (Matt. 22: 35-40). If this principle were accepted and practically applied, every law of God protective of the social rights and interests of men would be fulfilled in love, and all selfishness and injustice cease; for no person would murder, steal, commit adultery, bear false witness, or covet another's possessions, who loved his neighbor as himself (Rom. 13: 10).

Upon these three cardinal principles enunci-

ated by the Christ he founded a social polity
which is called his Church. They were not,
however, original with the man Jesus (John 8:
28), all fundamental principles being eternal in
God, but enunciated and practically applied by
him in the Church (Eph. 1: 22; 3: 10; 5: 27;
Col. 1: 18, 24). As he was the Word—the expression in humanity of Sonship in God—so
was his Church the Word or expression on
earth of the social polity eternal in heaven, and
was called by him the Kingdom of God (Luke
4: 43; Acts 1: 3)—at first purely idealistic,
coming not by observation (Luke 17: 20), and
having objectively no realization in a sinful and
selfish world, yet finding expression in our outward lives to the degree we become conscious
of it and practice its principles in the adjustment of our social relations with God and men.
And to all, however few in number, and however otherwise imperfect, who respond in heart,
mind, and soul to the gospel of glory to God in
the highest, and on earth peace, good will toward man, it is Salvation, well-being, complete
redemption from social thralldom, and the Gate
of entrance to the Kingdom of God.

Now that this definition of the Church—of
a brotherhood designed to cultivate, illustrate,
and practically apply the principles of the gos-

pel in the world, whereby the law is fulfilled in
love—is the true one, cannot be reasonably
questioned. In fact all Christian denominations recognize in theory its communistic idea,
howbeit few if any have attempted to define
and illustrate in practice what this idea is, but
have limited it to a community in creeds, in
sacraments, or in systems of worship. All of
these, however true or essential to its organization, are merely speculative or conventional
and totally inadequate to the fulfillment of the
law in love, unless accompanied and illustrated
by a community of unselfish social interests.
No man, or congregation of men, can love God
except he love his brother also (1 John 4: 7,
20, 21). Nor can we love our brother except
we love also our Father in heaven; for all
ideas of kinship and social community must be
derived from Fatherhood (Mal. 2: 10; Matt.
25: 34–46; Jas. 2: 15, 16; 1 John 3: 17).

The community of the Church is intended to
illustrate the very highest conception of paternal, filial, and fraternal love, and is described
as the Fold (John 10: 16), and the Household
(Matt. 10: 25) of God, and all its members as
branches of one Vine (John 15: 5). Hence, it
is impossible that its ideal should be realized in
the world—should represent the glory of God,

peace on earth, and good will toward men—except there be unity in all interests and possessions, as of parents and children in one family. Accordingly we find that the first church organized at Jerusalem represented such unity, and was wholly communistic,—that "the multitude of them that believed were of one heart and one soul; neither said any of them that aught of the things he possessed was his own, but they had all things common."

This community of possessions, however, was wholly voluntary (Acts 5: 4; 11: 29)—the idea of compulsion being necessarily inconsistent with the fulfillment of the law in love— although essential to the constitution of the church. Except every member, according to his ability, bestowed his goods upon his fellow-members as they had need, he could not be a member, his ability and need being rightly estimated in the unselfish conscience of the Church. But every member, and indeed the church itself, necessarily leads two lives—the one in the world, wherein he is subject to the law and the necessities pertaining thereto, and the other in the Kingdom of God wherein he fulfills the law in love. Under the law it is necessary and right that he should hold his possessions by legal titles and in his own name, and he may and should accumulate and possess this world's goods so far as he can do so lawfully and justly—it being utterly vain and foolish to attempt to practice an equal community of possessions among men more or less selfish, dissipated, and criminal, who are unwilling even to attempt to fulfill the law in love. But in the true church, wherein all are brethren and members of one household, he cannot selfishly regard his possessions as exclusively his own, but must share with his fellow-members as they have need the usury of his talents (Matt. 25 : 14–29). In the one case he renders unto Cæsar the things that are Cæsar's, and in the other unto God the things that are God's (Matt. 22 : 21).

Now while there was no compulsion whatever in the original church, no person being compelled to become a member or remain a member, yet so long as one was a member he was in perfect subjection to its authority. The Kingdom of God is an absolute monarchy, in complete subjection to him ; and as the Church was fashioned in the likeness of that Kingdom, and the two are one, it is also in complete subjection to its Founder (Eph. 1 : 22, 23), the Perfect Man, the Son of God, even as the Son is in complete subjection to the Father (John

5: 30; 1 Cor. 15: 28). Yet as a Kingdom
ruled in righteousness is ruled in love, and as
our subjection to the church is wholly voluntary, that the law may be fulfilled in love, such
subjection is perfect freedom, and the idea of an
absolute monarchy does not differ in principle
from that of a government administered by a
King ruling in righteousness (Isa. 32: 1; John
18: 37), or of one ruling by the people and for ·
the people (Acts 1 : 23--26). So while there is
absolute authority in the true church, exercised
primarily by the Christ, and secondarily by the
apostles and other ministers chosen by the
people under his direction, there is no law,
each member, so long as he is a member, being
in voluntary subjection to the higher powers
(Rom. 13: 1). The sacraments so called in our
day,—which are the symbols, or " outward
and visible signs of inward and spiritual grace,"
and by which fellowship is secured and made
manifest—are in the place of law, and represent
the covenant whereby each member is pledged
to obedience by the fulfillment of the law in
love, is promised redemption from all social oppressions (Matt. 1: 28; John 8: 32, 36; Gal.
4: 26), and ultimately resurrection to a glorified and immortal life (John 3: 15; 11: 25;
Rom. 8: 18; 1 Cor. 15: 54).

BOOK SECOND.

THE GATE CALLED BEAUTIFUL.

"And a certain man, lame from his mother's womb, was carried, whom they laid daily at the gate of the temple which is called Beautiful, to ask alms of them that entered into the temple."—Acts 3: 2.

PROLOGUE.

AN open gate is a means of ingress to any place or condition, or of egress therefrom ; or, if closed and bolted, the prevention of ingress or egress. It represents alike a privilege or a limitation of privilege; an opening through a barrier or the interposition of a barrier; a channel of communication between things without and things within, or a limitation of communication.

In nature all things, though mutually dependent, are protected by barriers furnished with gates, whereby they may be brought in contact with, or separated from, each other as convenience or necessity may require. Thus the eye, though a medium of communication between things without and things within, being a delicate organ and easily injured, is protected by a strong barrier of bone and muscle, and furnished with a gate which may be opened and shut at pleasure. No being could retain its distinctive character and use without bar-

113

riers for protection, nor could it receive or bestow its proper influences except such barriers
were furnished with gates. Indeed all things
would be wholly isolated, and would lose their
distinctive and relative character, place, and
condition, unless there were channels of communication, and in such case would cease to
exist since all are social in nature and mutually
dependent for their existence. The chain of
cause and effect, of demand and supply, of
variation and extension, which binds differing
beings in Unity, would be broken, and the
order and community of Being rendered impossible. Hence, while no being can be entirely and permanently isolated from commun-
ion with others, but must have points of possible
contact with them, whereby it may receive
what is essential to its existence and well-being,
and impart what is essential to the existence
and well-being of others, each must be protected from uncongenial intrusions. No one
being, in the natural and just order of beings,
can rightly be permitted to pass into the domain
of another, if it be injurious thereto ; and though
the two be mutually dependent, yet the degrees
of contact must be limited to mutual uses.
Thus the food which the hand ministers to the
stomach through the gateway of the mouth

may only be admitted thereto in the qualities
and quantities required, else both stomach and
hand would suffer injury.

What is true of our physical is true also of
our moral and intellectual natures. All the
functions and faculties of our social being need
protection, and would become enslaved, were
they not surrounded with barriers and furnished with gates which may be opened and
shut at will, so that one may not intrude upon
another to its detriment. And if there be a
heaven, a social order of perfect liberty, equality, and fraternity, from which all conditions of
sin, selfishness, and oppression are excluded, it
must be protected from the intrusions of sinful,
selfish, and oppressive spirits (Gen. 3: 24; 2
Chron. 23: 19; Ps. 118: 19, 20; Matt. 18: 3;
Luke 13: 24; Rev. 21: 27). None can be permitted to enter who are indisposed to love God
and their fellow-men; for otherwise the existence of a social condition of peace and brotherhood would be impossible. Nevertheless it
would itself represent a selfish condition, if it
were exclusive of any who, in the culture of
true religion, were disposed to fulfill the law in
love; and so its walls are furnished with gates
(Rev. 21: 12) whereby it may be brought into
contact with inferior conditions and exert its

influence upon them, and receive unto itself all congenial spirits.

It is not surprising, therefore, that the Temple, which was intended to illustrate and apply the principles of social order, as defined in the moral law, should have been surrounded with a wall furnished with gates, corresponding in number to the ten Articles of the law, whereby all persons obedient thereto might be admitted, and all others excluded; and though its purpose had been perverted—it having become a den of thieves, a medium of social oppression, a nurse of worldly pride and cupidity—it no doubt represented in theory the social polity of the Kingdom of God. Each of its gates was a symbol, not only of a privilege but also of a limitation of privilege, being designed to give entrance to all persons worthy of admission, and to exclude all unworthy. Its idea was precisely the same as that of the moral law it represented, which, while affirming a social right, decreed also the forfeiture of such right by any who should fail to recognize and respect it. It meant that an idolater, thief, or murderer, or any other trespasser upon social rights, should not be permitted to enter, while at the same time it gave entrance to all who were obedient to the law.

One of the ten gates was called Beautiful, and perhaps intended to represent the prophetic idealism associated with the anticipation of the coming Messiah. The psalms and prophecies of the Jewish scriptures abound in such poetic conceptions. Thus we read, "Lift up your heads, O ye gates, and be ye lifted up, ye everlasting doors, and the King of glory shall come in" (Ps. 24: 7; 118: 19, 20); "I will make thy windows of agates, and thy gates of carbuncles, and all thy borders of pleasant stones" (Isa. 54: 12; Ezek. 43: 4). That the gospel, which fulfills the law in love, should be thus idealized as a gate of beauty is both natural and practical—it being in fact the Beautiful Gate of entrance to the Kingdom of God, the heavenly Jerusalem (Gal. 4: 26; Rev. 3: 12).

Now every gate that God builds represents a right and the protection of that right. Indeed the idea of righteousness is identical therewith, for no right could exist except it represent a natural privilege or immunity under the protection of the law of God. It is predicated of the social nature of God, and as he is absolute, is eternal and invariable. As subjective, it is his consciousness and will; as objective, its expression is in our just relations to each other in outward things. Man, being in God's image, intuitively apprehends the idea of right to the degree of his development in conscience and will in harmony with the divine consciousness and will. Its spirit is justice and love; its purpose is beauty and joy; its operation is law and order. It is the principle of harmony in the limitless diversities that make up the unity of all beings in one Being, and is therefore in its true idea wholly social.

By human rights, therefore, we understand social privileges and immunities inherent in our nature of the social nature of God, which are essential to our well-being, and are either natural or acquired—derived of the nature of God, or justly acquired by the free exercise of our natural gifts. All are gateways or channels of communication between God and Man, and man and man, that, to the degree of our ability to give and receive, we may each and all possess and enjoy all things in common.

PART I.

By liberty we understand the unrestricted possession, exercise, and enjoyment of all our natural and lawfully acquired rights. But as man is naturally and necessarily a social being, his freedom is also social, and may not be exercised by one irrespective of the rights of another. It is impunity in obedience to the law, but not in violation thereof. In fact it can exist only as a development of law, and may be possessed and exercised only in recognition thereof; for since law is the protection of rights, and one forfeits such protection by disobedience—is deprived of his rights if he trespasses upon another's rights, and is placed under duress—his freedom can only be exercised in observance of the law which confers it upon him. And as law evolves and develops necessity, freedom consists in our possession of, or ability to obtain, the necessities of life. Thus to be free to move we must be furnished with organs essential to motion ; or if we are hungry

119

or naked, we must be able to procure food or
dress. Hence freedom cannot be impunity in
dissipation of necessities, or independence of
anything essential to our well-being. Every
necessity, representing, as it does, a medium
whereby freedom may be exercised, is essential
thereto. It means that we may live, but not
squander our means of livelihood—our food in
gluttony, our drink in drunkenness, our dress
in extravagance, or any other necessity in excess thereof; may move, but not intrude upon
forbidden grounds. In fact, law, freedom, and
necessity are one, and neither can rightly exist
without the others any more than an effect
without its cause, or a whole without its parts.
Hence, if society be free, it must be organized
lawfully, and must cultivate all necessities of
body and mind essential to freedom, and those
only; and each individual therein must be obedient to social laws, and must contribute to
social necessities according to his ability.

Now as all things of God must have a true
method or way of existence, and if, as we believe, the true method or way in which society
should be organized is represented in the moral
law fulfilled by compulsory processes so far as
is necessary, and in love so far as men are
disposed or can be persuaded to voluntary

obedience, it is plain that the true method or way of the development of social freedom is in the culture of obedience and love. Yet while the moral law and the gospel are recognized in all the more enlightened communities of our day as the true theories of social order, society is far from free. While the more flagrant and despotic forms of oppression have been put away, others more subtle but not less destructive of human rights, and parasitic to a highly cultured but perverted social condition, have been evolved and developed. Extremes of riches and poverty, of refinement and brutality, of learning and ignorance, of ease and drudgery, of virtue and vice, and the natural sequences thereof—of loathsome and tormenting diseases and infirmities both of body and mind—are peculiar to our present civilization. Shall we conclude then, that a high degree of culture in the enlightenment of true religion in one member or class of society is necessarily accompanied with a corresponding brutality in another?—that one must be illiterate that another may be learned? that one must be poor that another may be rich?—or that one must be enslaved that another may be free? This cannot be, if we have in common one Father in heaven, who has bestowed equal natural rights on all his children, and has equally imparted to all natural aspirations for knowledge, riches, and freedom. And yet—taking, as we must and should, the world as it is, not as it should be—we are compelled to admit that social evils whereby our freedom is limited are natural incidents of the false culture of true religion as taught in the law and the gospel; for such religion, being only a light shining in darkness (Isa. 9 : 2 ; Matt. 4 : 16), must render by contrast the surrounding darkness the more intense, and may itself, to the degree of our selfishness, be perverted to unnatural uses by revealing opportunities of evil not before conceived of in our ignorance. As without increase in knowledge there could be no greater subtleties of evil disclosed, and without law there could be no transgressions of the law (Rom. 7 : 7), so without the gospel there could be no perversions of the gospel (1 Pet. 2 : 16). As the Christian religion is but partially applied, it is also partially perverted; and, as the better anything is the worse it inevitably becomes by perversion, so in society, while accepting the gospel in theory, yet failing to apply its principles in practice, new and greater social evils are developed thereby than could otherwise exist. Nevertheless, our only possible increase in freedom lies in our culture of true religion ; for while its perversion produces bondage, yet in its right use is presented our only hope of redemption from social oppression. Thus, a slave may be personally better off as a slave than as a freeman, since he may, if set free, pervert his liberty to indulgence in vice or crime, yet by freedom only is it possible for him to attain a nobler manhood.

While, therefore, our primary efforts in the culture of true religion should be exerted to the promotion of a larger liberty, we must not forget that we can be free only so far as we make good use of our freedom. We must not be too precipitate in abandoning the restrictions of the law for the freedom of the gospel—not as if in our present imperfections and limitations we had already attained or were already perfect (Phil. 3: 12)—lest our liberty in the gospel become only license, and develop social anarchy. The precept of the Christ addressed to his disciples, that they should not resist evil (Matt. 5: 39), applied only to the members of his Church in their social relations with each other, and not to the world; for he came not to destroy the law, and if evil in a sinful world were not resisted the law would be destroyed.

Now as the Ten Commandments represent all

the natural and lawfully acquired rights of man, and as true freedom is the free exercise and enjoyment of such rights, we may define thereby all the primary elements of freedom. Moreover, so far as cultured by the law, the privilege of entrance to the Temple through its ten gates, each representing a right affirmed by the law, was a symbol of freedom. And as the gate called Beautiful represented the prophetic and highest ideal of religion—of the law fulfilled in love—the Christian religion is our highest conception of freedom. The same ideal is illustrated in the parable of the sheepfold. Our Lord declares that he himself is the door by which his sheep are permitted to enter and find protection, and by which they may go out and find pasture—protection in their natural rights, and freedom to procure a livelihood by their own industry. All who seek to enter by some other way—to secure protection in any other way than by obedience to the principles of the law and the gospel—are thieves and robbers.

Yet the fact that social freedom, like a gate, is necessarily restrictive and limited to mutual uses, renders it possible, when the door by which such restriction and limitation is secured is under control of selfish men, to make the fold a medium of oppression—a prison or a den of thieves. Thus it was when Peter and John went up to the temple at the hour of prayer, that, while the poor beggar was excluded, thieves and robbers were admitted. The letter of the law had been preserved, but its spirit and purpose were destroyed. Thus the law reads, " Thou shalt not steal "—that is, shalt not deprive another of his natural and justly acquired possessions,—but the demons of selfishness and pride that take possession of the human heart had taken possession also of the Temple, and had fortified themselves therein, having perverted the law to the protection of riches unnaturally and unjustly acquired. Indeed every thief who has acquired his possessions by robbing or enslaving others, compelling them to devote their natural gifts of God and the increase of their labors to his exclusive use, making them poor that he may be rich, brutish that he may be refined, ignorant that he may be learned, drudges that he may be indolent, is prone to justify himself by the letter of the law which he himself has violated in spirit (Rom. 2 : 21, 23). Being in possession of property and privilege that he has acquired by unjust means—by the oppression of others— he claims protection in the law, saying to the poor whom he has robbed, when they seek to recover their rights of life, liberty, and the pursuit of happiness, "Thou shalt not steal."   No person who is unwilling to confer freedom on others is himself entitled to freedom; nor, if he be unwilling that the rights of others be protected, is he entitled to protection in his own rights.

But we may not assume that, because others are in possession of greater wealth than we, they are necessarily thieves; or that capitalists who have laborers under their control are necessarily tyrants; for they may have acquired their possessions by the legitimate exercise of their natural rights—by the freedom and privilege conferred in the right use of their natural and justly acquired gifts of God—although they would be thieves and tyrants if they did not use their riches for the promotion of the best interests of others as well as of their own.   In short, if the law be fulfilled in selfishness and not in love, it becomes simply a refined system of oppression, enabling the rich to enslave the poor; and as selfishness is universal in a sinful, world, all laws are more or less perverted to selfish purposes.   "What then? Is the law sin? God forbid. Nay, I had not known sin but by the law; for I had not known lust, ex-

cept the law had said, Thou shalt not covet."
The law teaches us what our rights are, and
that trespassing thereon is sin, and is, therefore,
an inestimable blessing if fulfilled both in letter
and spirit. Without such knowledge we should
in our ignorance of human rights have continued to trespass thereon, and as a natural and
inevitable sequence of such ignorance poverty,
thralldom, and death would have continued to
reign as they reigned from Adam to Moses
(Rom. 5: 14). Hence, we must conclude that
social freedom is possible of attainment only by
obedience to the law and its fulfillment in love
(John 8: 32; 2 Cor. 3: 6; Gal. 4: 3-5; 5: 3-6).

While, therefore, the law is essential to freedom, it cannot itself alone redeem a selfish and
sinful world from bondage, and if perverted becomes a bulwark of oppression. And no doubt
it is so perverted in our day that most men
have become enslaved thereby—enabling, as it
does, a few to become rich, and compelling the
masses to remain poor. Can we wonder, then,
that so many have come to regard all laws enacted for the protection of social rights as
devices of the rich for the enslavement of the
poor, and would destroy all laws human or
divine that they may attain redemption from
social oppression? But the principles—if we

may call them principles—of anarchy or nihil-
ism are not such as evolve and develop social
freedom, but are hostile thereto except they
represent the law fulfilled in love; for laws
natural and moral are the sources of freedom,
and without such laws there could be no natural
or justly acquired rights. Hence, when St.
Paul asserts (Rom. 6: 14) that the true Christian is no longer under the law, he does not
mean that the law has been abolished, but has
been fulfilled—obeyed voluntarily through love
of and devotion to the principles of truth and
freedom asserted in and maintained by the law.
It may be said, however, that all civil laws are
unjust, being enacted by the rich for the enslavement of the poor; which is no doubt true
so far as such laws represent the corruption
and perversion of the laws of God; and as
selfishness is universal all civil laws are no
doubt leavened therewith. Still, as our nature
is not utterly depraved and may be improved
by art, so also may the corrupt social systems
we have constructed be reformed. Plainly
civil laws cannot be reformed by their destruction any more than Cain or Saul could have
been reformed had they been put to death;
howbeit both sinful society and the laws it
makes will be destroyed, and in the dispensa-

tion of God's providence, often have been, when found incapable of improvement.

While, therefore, there is a hope or possibility of increased social freedom, we must render unto Cæsar the things that are Cæsar's, and unto God the things that are God's (Matt. 22: 21). In fact, we cannot do otherwise, in so selfish and sinful a world as this, than appeal unto Cæsar for the protection of the rights and liberties we do possess, which would be utterly extirpated with the extirpation of civil laws. This necessity, however, of submission to Cæsar is not a sufficient apology for the selfishness and cupidity by which one class of society is enslaved by another; for any person who does not do all he can to reform the civil laws, and right the wrongs which others suffer, is personally responsible therefore, and is justly reckoned as a tyrant, thief, and robber.

But how, it may be asked, can we submit to be wronged by an unjust and oppressive social system, and at the same time defend and exercise our natural rights? How can we consent to be slaves and at the same time assert and maintain our rightful freedom? This is the great social problem of our times, and the one which the gospel of the Christ alone can solve —although not even the gospel can solve it ex-

cept to the degree we accept and practically
apply its principles. Nay, we do not hesitate
to affirm that omnipotence is incapable of conferring freedom upon any who do not accept
and practice the moral and religious principles
from which alone freedom is evolved and developed. Even the Christ was compelled to
submit to Cæsar until his earthly mission was
completed on the cross. Like him we should
be "wise as serpents and harmless as doves"
(Matt. 10: 16); and if we follow his counsels,
no doubt the mammon of unrighteousness (Luke
16: 9) may be made the friend of the poor, and
even Cæsar the defender of our rights and
liberties.

What is true in theory is the moral law practically interpreted by the gospel; and what is
true in practice is the application of the law to
the establishment of free institutions as we are
able to bear them. No doubt it is useless, as
affirmed in our institutes of civil law, to legislate now for society as it should be hereafter;
that is, to attempt to establish and enforce
principles of which the masses are ignorant and
not yet able to bear them; but we should not
infer that we can do nothing for society as it
should be—for the promotion of a larger liberty
—because all are selfish; for to the degree we

know the truth, the truth may be practically applied, and to the degree it is so applied will it set us free. Said the Christ to his disciples: "I have yet many things to say unto you, but ye cannot hear them now, howbeit when he, the Spirit of Truth, is come, he will guide you into all truth, and will show you things to come." Except to the degree we understand what the true theory of freedom is, it is useless to attempt to legislate for its promotion. Yet no person is a true follower of the Christ, or a believer in his gospel of freedom, who does not both in religion and politics exert his utmost influence for the promotion and protection of the rights and liberties of his fellow-men. While opposing all socialistic theories other than the moral law and the gospel, which interpret freedom as impunity from all restraint in our selfish condition, we should favor all measures that tend to limit and restrain cupidity and oppression. Indeed there can be no doubt that if the churches were not corrupted by worldliness, politics would be so leavened and purified with the Spirit of Truth that most of the many and great refinements and subtleties of cruelty and oppression incident to our present civilization would be immediately suppressed.

Now that the gospel of the Christ is the gospel of freedom, and that it was intended to be practically applied and illustrated by the church in this life that we may be eased of our burdens here, and also prepared for admission to the Kingdom of God in which all are free, cannot be reasonably questioned. As religion is unity, and as true unity can exist only in just social relations, and just social relations only in freedom, it is evident that if Christianity be the true religion it must represent both unity and freedom. In fact it is expressly declared that the mission of the Christ as defined by the prophets, was to proclaim liberty to the captive, to break every yoke, and let the oppressed go free. He also himself declared, when he practically entered upon his mission, that he came to set at liberty them that are bruised. And surely he would not have declared, "if the Son shall make you free ye shall be free indeed," or have invited all who were weary and heavy laden to come unto him for rest, if his mission were not to establish social freedom. "Our citizenship," says St. Paul, "is in heaven" —that is, the Church on earth, if uncorrupted, represents and is the Kingdom of God; and if we are all true members thereof we are members of that Kingdom, and are accounted as already free (1 Cor. 7: 22; Gal. 4: 31).

We must, therefore, as the Christ teaches, and in imitation of his example, recognize and practically illustrate in the Church the Fatherhood of God and the Brotherhood of Man, or we cannot attain unto the glorious liberty of the sons of God (Rom. 8: 21). All other social theories, brotherhoods, unions, societies, or orders, unless founded on the principles of the law and the gospel, are heresies, wells without water, clouds that are carried with a tempest, promising liberty while they are themselves the servants of corruption (2 Pet. 2: 1, 17, 19).

PART II.

THE GOSPEL OF EQUALITY.

WHILE liberty is the primary requisite to social redemption, such redemption being possible only to the degree we are free to use and enjoy all our natural and lawfully acquired rights and possessions, it is not the only requisite. One may be a free man under the law, and yet have very little to possess or enjoy, and very little opportunity or capacity to acquire riches; in which case his freedom would avail him little to the promotion of his social well-being. Thus this poor beggar whom Peter and John encountered at the gate called Beautiful was free so far as the law itself could confer freedom, and yet was unable to attain social redemption. The gate was open, but he was not permitted to enter on account of his infirmity.

Though a slave be set free from the legal control of his master, his freedom would prove only a curse, if he be unable to appreciate or avail himself of it to the promotion of his personal well-being. So also a free system of government—one founded on the letter of the moral law, and asserting the right of every individual to life, liberty, and the pursuit of happiness—will inevitably become a system of oppression if its laws are not fulfilled in love— if the freedom secured permits any individual or class selfishly to accumulate wealth without restriction, and compels the masses to devote the fruits of their industry to the enrichment of the few. Any system, in fact, under which one man or class is permitted to possess and control to his exclusive use more than his just portion of the natural gifts of God by which life is sustained and wealth accumulated—land, water, air, and light, and even the personal gifts of body and mind whereby we live and move and are enabled to create riches for ourselves by our own industry—practically becomes a licensed system of oppression; for, however true in the letter, it is a thief and murderer in spirit—a wolf in sheep's clothing.

In short, so far as human rights are selfishly interpreted, freedom becomes a farce—construed unsocially to mean the private right of any individual or class to promote his own interests regardless of the interests of others, whereas it is in fact his right and ability only to promote his interests equally and in common with all other members of society. That is, freedom is social, not selfish. What advantage is it to be protected in our rights by the letter of the law, if we are already deprived of our rights?—permitted to become rich, if we have no opportunity to accumulate riches?—to live, move, and have our being, if the fruits of our industry be consumed mostly by others, and the best we can do is to secure a scant livelihood for ourselves and families by constant and excessive toil? Plainly as "faith without works is dead," so is freedom without equality (Gal. 5: 13)—without an opportunity at least to make oneself equal with others. "If a brother or sister be naked and destitute of daily food, and one of you say unto them, depart in peace, be ye warned and filled, notwithstanding ye give them not those things which are needful to the body; what doth it profit?" (Jas. 2: 15, 16). Hence, if the gospel of the Christ be the true religion, and represents the true idea of social unity and freedom, so is it the gospel of equality—that which not only bestows freedom, but also the opportunity of its use and enjoyment. By equality we mean equity, and by equity equal opportunities for acquirement, possession and enjoyment.

Now the gate called Beautiful was a symbol of freedom so far as the law could confer it, and, in like sense, of equality. It meant the equal protection of the natural and lawfully acquired rights of all, and the free exercise thereof; and as the sole condition of entrance was obedience to the moral law, all who were obedient were equally protected in their possessions and privileges. But it did not mean that all were made equal with each other in their natural and personal gifts and possessions, for such equality was impossible in the nature of things. An obedient child, for example, though permitted to enter, could not thereby be made equal with its parents in authority, experience, or knowledge; nor one man physically weaker than another equal therewith in strength; nor one poor in purse, intelligence, or moral and emotional endowments with one rich therein (Matt. 6: 27; Rom. 12: 6-8). Such equality could not be immediately and arbitrarily conferred and enforced by the law— would in fact, even if it were possible to enforce it, be inequality, injustice, and oppression, taking that which rightfully belonged to one and conferring it upon another. No person who came to the gate seeking entrance to the privileges of the temple, was deprived of anything

he naturally and lawfully possessed—the sole
condition of entrance being obedience to the
law. Yet the right to enter secured by obedience, was the first and essential requisite of
equality—it being self-evident that social
equality would be impossible in a society in
which murder, theft, covetousness, and other
transgressions of human rights were permitted.
As anarchy without true religion is not freedom,
neither is it equality ; and if, as we have seen,
obedience to the law is essential to freedom, so
also must it be to equality. Indeed to reduce,
either by legal or brute force, the superior to a
level with the inferior—to limit the just rights
and privileges of one in order to bestow unjust
rights and privileges upon another, or to compel
one to open his gate to the admission of the
thief and robber, or any other uncongenial element of society, so far from being social equality, would be the worst conceivable oppression
and inequality—would be compelling us to cast
our pearls to swine (Matt. 7 : 6).

Moreover, it is manifestly impossible, useless,
or wasteful to bestow upon any person more
than he has capacity to receive, or is disposed
to use for the promotion of his real interests.
Thus, a child cannot come into possession of
manly thoughts and acquirements until it be-

comes a man and puts away childish things
(1 Cor. 13: 11); and it would be a waste of
treasure to bestow it upon one prodigal and
dissipated.

But while the true idea of equality is not
properly defined as the even distribution of our
possessions and acquirements of body and mind, ·
it does mean a social condition in which all
share equally with each other in opportunities
for improvement, possession, and enjoyment—
a commonwealth of mutual interests and ad-
vantages—a family, brotherhood, congregation
or church, in which all members are of one
heart and one soul, and no one member calls
aught of the things he possesses exclusively his
own, but inclusively his in common with all
other members.

To secure such equality each must first attain
freedom by obedience to the moral law—that is,
must be a moral man, so that, if equality be
conferred upon him, he will respect the rights
of others; and second, must fulfill the law in
love—that is, not because he is compelled to do
so, or merely for his own self-interest, but
through devotion to right principles and the
unselfish love of God and man. As no man
who loves God and his fellow-men could either
desire to be inferior to others, or that others

should be inferior to himself, every person who
seeks to fulfill the law in love seeks to promote
social equality—not by either debasing others
to an inferior social position, or by exalting
himself above others, but by striving to promote the well-being of all.   Hence, as the fulfilling of the law in love is Christianity, no
person can be a member of the true church who
does not seek to promote social equality—first,
by becoming equal in his industry and thrift
with all other members who are superior to
himself in good gifts, and second, by helping
to make all others who are inferior equal with
himself (Isa. 35: 3, 4; Heb. 12: 12, 13).   Indeed, the moment one becomes a true member
of the true church is he placed in a position of
equality with all other members, having thereby
become free therein from all injustice and oppression, and given to the degree of his ability
to receive every opportunity and privilege for
acquirement, possession, and enjoyment which
any and all other members possess.   Even as
our faith is counted unto us for righteousness
(Gen. 15: 6; Ps. 106: 31) while we are still
otherwise imperfect, so may equality be im-
puted to all true members of the church, however unequal they may otherwise be in natural
or acquired gifts, or however small and feeble

the congregation in numbers and resources.
Thus the man Jesus, though despised and persecuted on earth, yet, being in the form of God,
thought it not robbery to be equal with God
(Phil. 2: 6); and while no man can be above
his master (Matt. 10: 24, 25), he may be as his
Master—nay, perfect, as his Father in heaven
is perfect. The equality which Jesus claimed
with the Father was free and equal participation with him in his limitless glory, life, riches,
knowledge, authority and power; not, however, that he sought to be personally as great as
the Father, as in the nature of things sonship,
being secondary to fatherhood, dependent
thereon, and existing therein, is subordinate
thereto—and he expressly declares his Father
to be greater than he (John 14: 28)—but that
he was one with Him in interests, and therefore
through free and limitless participation was
equal with him,—even as every son, though not
as great as his father, naturally partakes
equally with him in all his possessions. Social
equality, then, is not equality in personal
merits, that being impossible in the nature of
things, but in the use and enjoyment of each
other's merits according to our abilities. It is
the "wedding garment," in which all must be
clothed who are permitted to partake in

common of social privileges (Matt. 22: 11), however unequal they may be in their natural gifts and acquirements, and in the seats they properly occupy (Luke 14: 10). Otherwise social chaos would ensue, and there could be no authority or moral law, each individual, however deficient in culture, regarding himself of equal merit with any other, however superior.

It is, therefore, taught in the gospel as an essential principle of freedom and equality that all members of the church must be subject to the higher powers (Rom. 13: 1-7); "for there is no power but of God, and whosoever resisteth the power resisteth the ordinance of God." While every true member is a power of God, and there is no limit placed upon his acquirements, he is always himself subject to a higher power, "which is a minister of God to him for good."

Each person must occupy the position to which his merits entitle him and as these increase he will be called to come up higher. Such, no doubt, is the Kingdom of God—a social condition of limitless increase in knowledge, happiness, and power. No person should think of himself more highly than he ought to think (Rom. 12: 3-5), "for as we have many members in one body, and all members have not the same office, so we, being many, are one body in Christ, and all members one of another."

But while in a condition of social equality one is superior to another in merits, and is thereby entitled to exercise a greater authority, yet all are subject one to another (1 Pet. 5: 5) —the superior being the greater servant, greater responsibilities being imposed upon him (Matt. 23: 11). Thus one who is rich in this world's goods is required to distribute among his poorer brethren (Matt. 19: 21; 1 Tim. 6: 18); one that is strong, to support the weak (Rom. 15: 1); one that is wise and learned, to instruct the foolish and unlearned (2 Tim. 2: 2); one that is happy, to contribute to the happiness of others (John 15: 11; 17: 13; 2 Cor. 1: 24)—thereby sharing his gifts with other members of the household as they have need (Acts 2: 45; Gal. 6: 10).

Another principle of equality is that no member of the church should owe another anything, except to love him; and for this reason, that that debt is an obligation of the law, and when the law is fulfilled in love all such obligations are discharged (Matt. 6: 12; Rom. 13: 8). Every debt, except of love, is bondage, and there can be no Kingdom of God on earth except to the degree its members are forgiven their debts, and have forgiven their debtors. All interests being in common, the debts and credits of each become those of all, and are thereby extinguished; and though one receives more than he gives, yet if he gives all he is capable of bestowing he is not a debtor; or if he gives more than he receives he is not made a creditor thereby, having done no more than love requires. Thus while the child receives from its parents more than it can bestow upon them, yet if they love one another there is no debt or credit incurred. By love is not meant simply an emotion, although it develops pure emotion, but a religious sense of duty and mutual obligations, evolved and developed of our social nature, which leads us to do unto others as we would they should do unto us. Pure love is more than unselfish, and impels us to sacrifice our personal interests, if need be, to the promotion of the well-being of others who are less fortunate than we—to sell all that we have, if need be, to give to the poor, thus making ourselves poor that others may be rich—howbeit every sacrifice of love makes us ultimately the richer therefor (Matt. 5 : 3 ; 19 : 21). Thus, however rich a man may be, yet if he becomes a member of a true church, in which all share equally in the increase of each other's possessions, his riches are increased thereby, however poor his fellow-members may be ; for equality in the church practically puts each member in possession of the combined riches of all, and as the church is the household of God, its power to possess is unlimited.

This reasoning, however, will not be convincing if we judge simply by appearances, but is absolutely conclusive if we judge righteous judgment (John 7 : 24). Appearances are deceptive because our eyes are full of the motes of selfishness, and these render that which is righteous—that which is for our best interests—seemingly subversive thereof. To judge righteous judgment—to understand what is really for our best interests—we must cast out from our eyes these motes of selfishness, and look upon each other with pure eyes of love—without dissimulation (Rom. 12: 9)— not greedy eyes, seeking only our own (1 Cor. 13 : 5).

Now, in order to determine accurately what are our own best interests, we must have a right idea of riches, and of the relative values of the differing kinds thereof to each other; for otherwise we may be satisfied with those of inferior value, which perish in the using.

Plainly the value of riches is determined by the blessings derived therefrom, either material or spiritual—food, clothing, shelter, strength, health, knowledge, life, power, joy; and by the greatness and durability of such blessings. In themselves they have no value more than talents laid up in a napkin or a tree barren of fruit, but from their increase they become the source of all good things (Deut. 16 : 15 ; Col. 2 : 19). But if such increase is derived by oppressing the poor, it renders our riches not only valueless, but a curse rather than a blessing (Prov. 22 : 16 ; Rev. 3 : 17), and for this reason, that they are perverted to selfish purposes, and selfishness is the parasitic worm which smites and destroys all blessings as it destroyed Jonah's gourd. Our social nature forbids that we should enjoy the increase of riches, except to the degree we share equally, that is justly, therein, for otherwise they are consumed by moths or rust, or stolen by thieves (Job. 13 : 28 ; Matt. 6 : 19 ; Jas. 5 : 1-3). In a world full of moths, rust, and thieves we cannot and ought not to bestow on others more than they are capable of making good use of, and are justly entitled to receive, yet in the true church, in which all are brethren, and selfishness, together with the evil parasites selfishness produces, is excluded, each may enjoy not only the full increase of his own riches, but also that of each other member. In fact, it is not possible, except in a very limited and transient sense, to become rich in any other social condition than that in which the law is fulfilled in love ; for the law must be fulfilled, and if not in love must be in selfishness, and if in selfishness, all good gifts sooner or later are consumed and destroyed by parasites. And we are selfish if we are unwilling that others who are willing to help themselves, and are equally obedient to the laws of God in letter and spirit, should have equal opportunities with ourselves for the acquirement of riches.

Doubtless no person will question that all good gifts come from God (Jas. 1: 17), or that we can give only as we have received from him ; but it is as certainly true that we can receive only as we give (Luke 6: 38), for if we fail to give as we have received we shall lose that we have gained (Mark 8: 35). Judging by appearances, and blinded by selfishness, we are likely to regard this as untrue, it being a matter of common observation that those who are too selfish to give as they receive appear to accumulate riches, and logically it would seem certain that the more we give the less we have.

Yet a moment's reflection is conclusive that the propositions of the Christ are both theoretically and practically true; for if our very nature and being are social, anything in conflict therewith is destructive thereof; and as the value of riches is determined by the blessings they bestow, they are certainly decreased in value to the degree they are hoarded or not used for the well-being of society, and rendered incapable of bestowing blessings. And they are certainly hoarded and wasted if one who is unwilling to give as he receives is permitted to accumulate them. Nor is the individual himself who thus acquires wealth able to enjoy it, but on the contrary is oppressed and cursed thereby (Rev. 3: 17; 18: 7, 8)—the same being true of nations as of individuals. Indeed, as asserted by the Christ, it is easier for a camel to go through the eye of a needle than for a rich man to enter into the Kingdom of God— that is, one who has laid up treasures for himself and is not rich toward God (Luke 12: 21); and one cannot be rich toward God without being rich toward his fellow-men. But on the other hand nothing is easier than for a rich man to become a true member of the Church, who, though rich in purse, is poor in spirit (Matt. 5: 1)—not satisfied with silver and gold only, but seeking to invest them in higher riches; for as we receive as we give, and one who is rich can give more easily and abundantly than one who is poor, he can the more easily enter into the Kingdom of God. To the rich man who thus makes good use of his talents shall be given, and he shall have more abundance; but to the poor man who doth not seek such increase shall be taken away that which he hath (Matt. 13: 12).

While nothing can be more certainly true than that we receive only as we give, yet so deceived are we by appearances, and so great is the deceitfulness of earthly riches held in the spirit of cupidity and worldly pride (1 John 2: 16), that doubtless most members of the church in our day regard equality therein, whereby all are permitted to share equally in each other's blessings, as unjust and impossible of practical realization. The idea, however, that any person however rich or poor can be wronged by loving his brethren in the church as himself is absurd and inconsistent with the purpose and spirit of the gospel. Says St. Paul: " If there be first a willing mind, it is accepted according to that a man hath, and not according to that he hath not. For I mean not that other men be eased and ye be burdened, but by an *equality*, that now at this time your abundance may be supply for their want, that their abundance also may be a supply for your want, that there may be equality. As it is written, He that had gathered much had nothing over; and he that had gathered little had no lack" (2 Cor. 8: 14). This is plainly a precise and true definition of social equality.

PART III.

THE GOSPEL OF FRATERNITY.

IN a literal sense brothers are sons of one father, and their association in one family constitutes a brotherhood; and as all men are children of God, all in like sense are brethren and members of one family (Job 33: 4; Acts 17: 25-29). Sonship in God is, therefore, Brotherhood in Man, and there can be no other, as there can be only one God and Father of all (Isa. 64: 8; Matt. 6: 9; John 5: 26),—howbeit, since every son and brother may become a father of a family, there may be an unlimited number of brotherhoods derived from, and comprehended in, the one Divine Family. But no brotherhood can be true and real except it be such both in letter and spirit (Rom. 9: 6-8) —in the image of the heavenly (1 Cor. 15: 49; 2 Cor. 3: 8)—all its members bound together in unity (John 11: 52; 17: 11; Eph. 4: 3, 13; Heb. 2: 11), and each loving his brother as himself. That is, so long and so far only as men recognize God as their Father, are obedi-

151

ent unto him (Isa. 38: 18, 19; 63: 8; 1 Pet.
1: 14, 15), and maintain right social relations
with each other, are they practically sons and
brothers (Matt. 5: 45; 13: 38; John 1: 12,
13; Rom. 8: 16; Gal. 3: 26; 1 John 3: 10).

As all men had sinned—that is, become disobedient to our common Father—(Eccl. 7: 20;
Rom. 3: 23), all, to the degree of their sinfulness, had become alienated from God (Eph. 2:
12), astray as sheep from his fold (Isa. 53: 6),
and the idea of Fatherhood in God and Brotherhood in Man almost oblitered from the popular conscience until the coming of the Christ,
whereby it has partially, and may be wholly,
restored.   Hence, as pointed out in the parable
of the Prodigal Son, our social redemption is
only possibly by our return to our Father's
house—by the restoration to our conscience
and life of the reality of our Sonship in God.
Such is the "Gospel of Fraternity"—obedience
to God, and peace and good will toward men.
Such was and is the mission of Jesus—the
social polity of his gospel—to seek for and
bring back to his Father's house all his brethren that had gone astray therefrom (John 10:
16).   Such is the meaning of atonement—the
reconciliation of men to God and to each other
(Matt. 5: 24; Rom. 5: 10; 2 Cor. 5: 18, 19;

Col. 1: 20, 21); and to this purpose both the Old and New Testament Scriptures are wholly devoted—the restoration of our lost Sonship in God and Brotherhood in Man. In fact, there can be no true religion other than that bond of love which binds all men to God and to each other; for otherwise we are naturally and of necessity selfish and unsocial, and our salvation —which is our social well-being—is impossible.

If then, as must have been rightly taught in the original Church, true membership therein secures our salvation (Acts 2: 47), every true church must represent a household of God, and must practically illustrate what a true brotherhood is—not simply by calling God our Father (Matt. 25: 40, 45; John 8: 41, 42), but by keeping his commandments. Nor by simply calling our fellow-members brethren (Matt. 5: 46, 47), for there is an endless number of brotherhoods, so-called, organized mostly for selfish or partisan purposes, but by striving to love them as ourselves, and doing unto them as we would they should do unto us. Men can of course combine together for any purpose, even for robbery and murder, or to make war by legal methods upon the rights and interests of others, and call such combination a brotherhood, but it is manifestly true that only so far as they

are united in obedience to God, and in the
spirit of mutual love, is there any real fraternity.   And as true religion is the bond of union
between God and Man, and men and men, it is
also manifest that there can be no true religion
except in the practical culture of fraternal relations (Rom. 12 : 10 ; 1 Thess. 4 : 9).

Now the Christ, as we have seen, asserted
the Fatherhood of God and the Brotherhood of
Man as principles essential to our social redemption ; and not only asserted these principles
but also taught how they may be practically
applied by a congregation of believers called a
church, a Kingdom of God on earth, wherein
all faithful members thereof may become free
from social oppression, equal one with another,
and sons and brothers in God's own household
(Rom. 8 : 14-17).

Like religion itself, therefore, fraternity
means unity—the joining together of many
differing personalities in one harmonious whole
(1 Cor. 10 : 17 ; Phil. 2 : 2)—in the fellowship
of the Son (1 Cor. 1 : 9), and with the Father
(1 John 1 : 3)—in citizenship (Eph. 2 : 19)—in
inheritance (1 Cor. 3 : 21, 22 ; Heb. 9 : 15)—in
mutual helpfulness and labors (Gal. 6 : 2 ; Phil.
4 : 3)—in sufferings (2 Tim. 1 : 8)—in consola-
tions (2 Cor. 1 : 6, 7)—in hopes and promises

(1 Cor. 9: 10; 2 Pet. 1: 4)—in glory (1 Pet. 5: 1)—in life (Rom. 6: 5).

Whatever exists must be manifested in combination with other things—all things being social in nature,—and must itself be composed of differing things which correspond with each other. By correspondences we mean harmonious variations which are essential to extension, continuity, and comprehension—parts in one whole which are complements of each other, each supplying what others lack, as the differing faculties essential to one mind; differing organs of one body; differing tints of one color; differing spheres of one universe. The proportion of differences in parts determines the character of the whole, and if the proportion be just, the correspondence will be perfect, and goodness, truth, and beauty will result therefrom. Otherwise the combination will produce chaos, anarchy, and decay.

Society being a structure, this law of correspondence determines its well-being. Although no two men can be precisely alike—else there would be no personal identity, one not being distinguishable from another, and the varieties of tastes, cultures, abilities, and callings essential to the vast and varied interests of society being lacking,—there may yet be harmony, all working for the common interests, each filling his natural and rightful position in relation to all other brethren, classes, or conditions (1 Cor. 1: 10). Thus there are differences in ages, experiences, possessions, abilities, pursuits, and duties, yet if all are bound together in the full recognition and protection of each other's rights as defined in the moral law, and fulfill the same in love as defined in the gospel, such social compact is the perfection of society, and would know no suffering or injustice (1 Cor. 12: 25-31).

While, therefore, it is quite proper and laudable that men of one calling should combine together in unions or brotherhoods for mutual culture and protection of their rights and interests, yet if they seek thereby to antagonize the interests of other callings—selfishly to promote their own interests to the detriment of others—they cease to be brotherhoods, and become enemies of society. Thus if farmers, merchants, manufacturers, mechanics, capitalists, laborers, or any other classes combine to obtain exorbitant prices, wages, profits, or privileges, they are irreligious, unsocial, and transgressors of the laws of God and the rights of man. Men must live together in the same world, and the better they can harmonize in their social interests the better will be the condition of each and all. All are made in one image, are of one flesh and blood, of like faculties, desires and necessities. The life of each is in the Life of one God and Father of all, as the branches of the vine in one Vine (John 15: 1-6; Acts 17: 26); and for one brother or brotherhood to war against the best interests of another is to render the one a thief and murderer, and the other a band of thieves and murderers (Gen. 4: 2, 8; Prov. 29: 24; 1 John 3: 15).

Fraternity is the goal of humanity,—the end of the law for righteousness (Rom. 10: 4-9)—the end of the Christian religion for our justification and reconciliation with God and Man, the fulfillment of all divinely inspired and prophetic ideals and conceptions of a power and glory to come—of a new heaven and a new earth, a new Jerusalem, and a new tabernacle of God with man, when all tears shall be wiped away. It is the mark set before us, the high calling of God our Father in his Son Christ Jesus our Brother (Phil. 3: 14). It is the perfection of our social nature and art—the law fulfilled in love. And the gate called Beautiful was the symbol of the practical method by which these divinely inspired social ideas might be realized by the exclusion of all unclean and selfish elements of society (2 Chron. 23: 19; 1 Cor. 6: 10), and the inclusion in one fold, and under one Shepherd, of all who would love God and their brother men. For necessarily the introduction into a sinful world of the Kingdom of God requires the separation of the unselfish from the selfish, it being impossible that these two elements should harmonize with each other. There must be a gate of separation so long as men are inharmonious in their social relations. The wheat must be winnowed from the chaff (Mal. 4: 1; Matt. 3: 12), the sheep separated from the goats. Truth cannot dwell in peace with falsehood, true riches with needless poverty, virtue with vice, temperance with dissipation, thrift with prodigality, or brotherly kindness with pride and envy. In short there can be no brotherhood except to the degree that all men are free and equal—free from sin and selfishness, and equal in rights and privileges through obedience to the moral law, and the fulfillment of the same in love.

The church of which Peter and John were members represented this ideal social compact and fraternity—the gathering together in one fold of all who were disposed to dwell together in peace and brotherhood. They were not, however, so impractical as to suppose that brotherhood could exist in a world universally selfish; yet believing in the principles of the law and the gospel, and inspired by the example of their Master, they had faith in its ultimate realization in the elimination of selfishness, and in the redemption of the whole human race from social thralldom. How could they indeed believe the law and gospel to be true if the universal brotherhood were impossible of realization as represented therein?—in the prophets who dreamed dreams of a glory to come, when men should beat their swords into plowshares, and their spears into pruning hooks, when nation should not rise up against nation any more, every man sit under his own vine and fig tree, and none should make them afraid?— under a God and Father of all, in a Kingdom of God, or in God with Man? No doubt selfishness is universal in depraved human nature, yet the nature thus perverted is nature still,—the natural and just sequence of a rational cause, —and is of God. The perversion of nature is not the destruction of nature, it being eternal in God's Nature, and in us as children of God, and despite its depravity in us it is not totally depraved.

In fact, strictly speaking, it is not depraved

at all, the depravity being in our perversion of
it to evil uses; and though it produces disease,
suffering, and death by such perversion, these
are the rational and just conditions resulting
from our transgressions of its laws—quite as
rational and just as the conditions of health,
joy, and life it develops when we are obedient
thereto. Disease and death mark the limits of
perversion and transgression, and are produced
by nature in the mercy of God that it may not
produce unending torments.

Hence, although men are in a greater or less
degree selfish, none who still live can be totally
selfish, and all may, if they will, be redeemed
and saved. As already shown, our nature and
art, if brought into harmony with the Divine,
produce unity, and in the perfection of society
are represented in a perfect brotherhood. But
as all men in the exercise of their free will cannot at once be brought into harmonious relations either by the compulsion of the law or the
persuasion of the gospel, the work of redemption must be begun by the separation of the
obedient from the disobedient. That is, while
the Kingdom of God may be established here,
when there are any who are willing to accept
it, it cannot include all so long as any reject it,
and there must be barriers erected between the

just and unjust, as there are between heaven and hell. Admission thereto must be conditional—effected through a gate; for otherwise there could be no protection of social rights.

The social ideal Peter and John represented was no longer simply a speculative theory, but one already partially realized in a congregation of believers who were of one heart and one soul, and called none of the things they possessed exclusively their own, but held them in common for the good of all. Indeed there can be no greater delusion than the idea that any true theory of reform is not practicable because the multitude are not ready to receive it; for this is to assume that righteousness is impossible, and that truth is dependent for its existence upon the popular will rather than upon the will of God. If men are not totally depraved, and if any there be who are desirous of improvement, every true social ideal is practicable, and its realization in outward life may be approximated by educational methods—by prophecy and instruction—whereby civil laws, however unjust, may be brought more and more into conformity with moral laws, and religion, however corrupt, into harmony with the gospel of love and reconciliation. Faith, hope, and love are innate in the social nature of Man, and cannot be utterly eliminated except he be himself blotted from existence. Hence, if evil motives be repressed and good motives developed and cultured, every man living will be found to be susceptible of improvement—receptive of higher inspirations and aspirations—so that while all men are sinful and selfish, it is always possible to introduce into the world the discipline of repentance—first by prophecy, and second by practical illustration in works meet for repentance. And if any person thinks this Gospel of Fraternity to be merely fanciful and impracticable, he is so selfish, so blinded by self-interest, that he cannot believe in the truth because it is the truth (John 8: 45)—being as he thinketh in his heart (Prov. 23: 7); and if he be professedly a Christian, he is practically if not consciously a hypocrite (Matt. 16: 3)—able to discern fair or foul weather, but not the signs of the times—natural, but not spiritual laws—what concerns his immediate, personal, and selfish interests, but not his future, social, and eternal welfare.

Peter and John were brethren—were of the church and were the church; and as such were free and equal—justly entitled to the privilege of entrance at the Gate to the Temple of God. But so corrupted was the society of their day,

and the true religion of the temple, that even
thieves and robbers were also permitted to
enter—howbeit these thieves and robbers were
obedient to the letter of the law. Very likely
Peter and John were the only brothers in spirit
and in truth who came up to the temple at this
hour of prayer; but their presence there served
to prevent the worship of the temple from becoming totally depraved, as had the presence
of the true prophets in preceding ages. And
being brothers, they were, like the Founder of
their order, also missionaries, and sought to
make all other men brothers, and to confer
upon them the same rights and privileges they
themselves enjoyed. This, however, could be
done only by closing the gate against thieves
and robbers, and opening it to others whom
thieves and robbers had excluded, both Jews
and Gentiles—which, considering they were
only two men of little social influence, would
seem a hopeless task. But being "wise as
serpents and harmless as doves," and conscious
that their Master was with them (Matt. 28 : 20;
Rom. 8 : 31), and that all things were possible
to those who believed and trusted in him
(Mark 9 : 23), they did not hesitate then and
there to attempt to apply practically their faith.
All they could do, however, at the time, so far

as regarded the thieves and robbers, was to enter with them into the temple in order to vindicate their own right to the enjoyment of its privileges, and to preserve, so far as their presence and influence could, the principles and purity of worship represented therein—hoping and believing that in time it might be converted from a den of thieves into a house of prayer. And to this end they sought to bring in with them those who, through physical or other infirmities, had been excluded or rendered incapable of entrance, and also by their example, brotherly kindness, preachings and exhortations to bring to repentance even the thieves and robbers, so that those who stole should steal no more, but rather working with their hands the things which were good, that they might have to give to them that needed (Eph. 4: 28). And no doubt, so far as the Church of our day has become corrupted and perverted to selfish, worldly, and vain purposes, a like method should be pursued. And that it has become thus perverted is evident, since it does not represent a brotherhood of social liberty, equality, and fraternity, and if not a brotherhood, is a den of thieves in the same sense that the temple was—that is, not necessarily in the letter, but in the spirit. Any society must be either one or the other—a brotherhood or a den of thieves; for it is plain that we cannot be brethren and at the same time selfish and unwilling to hold our possessions in common, so that those associated with us may participate in our privileges. Like the Temple—which was composed of Pharisees and Sadducees—the Church is divided into sects, hostile to each other, and each striving to win proselytes for the purpose of promoting its worldly and temporal interests—business or political (Matt. 23: 15). Like the temple also it is full of parasites —moths, rust, and thieves—those who subsist by catering to the vanities, superstitions, worldly pride, ignorance, dogmatic eccentricities and fancies, bigotries, and prejudices of its members. Each is more or less narrow, exclusive and intolerant of many who should be admitted, and inclusive of many who should be excluded —its conditions of admission being fixed by idosyncrasies of private opinions called articles of faith, rather than by the spirit of the gospel of the Christ, of godliness, brotherly kindness, and charity. Nevertheless, as the true Church is the Kingdom of God, and represents the one and only social compact and polity whereby the Fatherhood of God and the Brotherhood of Man can be realized, we should, like Peter and

John, enter in at its Beautiful Gate, and strive to fulfill the purpose of God therein. Corrupt as it now is, it is by no means utterly corrupt, but represents our highest religious and social culture, and our only hope of redemption from social thralldom, injustice, sin, and selfishness.

BOOK THIRD.

SOCIAL PROBLEMS.

" Who seeing Peter and John about to go into the Temple asked an alms."—Acts 3:·3.

PROLOGUE.

A HUMAN parasite is a person who derives his living wholly or in part from another's substance—literally, eats beside him, and at his cost. As all beings are necessarily social—living together in one world and deriving their subsistence from one God (Ps. 136 : 25, 26 ; Luke 20 : 38)—all are parasites at the Lord's table. Whether, therefore, our social condition be good or evil is determined by its parasitic character—that is, by how we live and eat together, whether harmoniously in proper recognition of each other's natural rights and necessities as children of one household, or otherwise regardless thereof.

But as this is confessedly a selfish and sinful world—by which we mean that while naturally social and mutually dependent we have become by transgression of God's laws unnaturally unsocial, not living and eating together harmoniously, but exclusive in spirit, each string to the degree of his selfishness to exclude others

169

from equal participation with himself in the privileges of the table our common Father has prepared for us all, or to shirk and shift the social responsibilities and duties in which each should share equally according to his abilities— the idea of parasite has come to be perverted in meaning, and used only in an evil sense to describe a being which, either from necessity, inability or indisposition, is unable or unwilling to labor for its own support, and subsists wholly or in part upon the labors and productions of others. And in this limited sense only shall we use the word.

As our interests are wholly social, all problems which concern our progress and reform are social problems; and as our social conditions must be determined by their parasitic developments, such problems necessarily involve inquiries into such developments as are evil in order that proper methods for their suppression may be devised and practically applied.

As accurately defined and classified by the Christ, evil parasites are of three varieties, the moth, rust, and thief (Matt. 6: 19)—that is, the consuming, dissipating, and plundering elements of society. These include all destructive elements, and were these removed, all social evils would cease to exist. Hence social prob-

lems are of three varieties : The Problem of
the Moth, The Problem of the Rust, and The
Problem of the Thief. These, however, are
closely related to each other, being of one kind,
and having a common source in sin and selfishness.

As man is superior to all other earthly creatures in his personal endowments of physical,
mental, and spiritual faculties, he is justly made
ruler over all (Gen. 1 : 28, 29). And being
ruler he is also responsible for their condition.
We may assume in fact that, as he is of more
value than the creatures which are subject to
him (Matt. 10 : 31), they were made for his use
—not, however, to their injury and destruction,
but for their well-being and preservation, even
as his body is made for the use of his spirit, so
that as he should be, so also may all things in
his world become ; for doubtless, by a just law
of Being, the better our condition, the better
will all things be which God has given us. Indeed it is quite certain that, as God's laws are
invariably rational and just, everything in our
environments is made to correspond with our
physical, mental, and moral conditions. That
is, as man is both an animal and a spirit, and as
the spirit is superior to the animal, the condition
of the one is determined by that of the other.

Hence we may assume that evil parasites in the natural world originate in, and are developed by, man's perverted conscience and will. In other words man's vitiated art, whereby his substance and nature have also become vitiated, has not only produced the destructive elements of society, but also all animal and vegetable pests which consume, waste, and plunder the fruits of the earth, and all fabrics which man's skill and industry have developed. That is, the earth is cursed for his sake (Gen. 3: 17, 18) and made to produce useless, poisonous, and destructive plants and animals. Any unrestrained evil thought, impulse or desire may, and naturally will, develop a correspondingly unhealthy condition of body; and as the body is wholly composed of substantives, such unhealthy condition will affect other material things with which it is in contact, and produce therein a like unhealthy condition. In this way man's environments in what we call the natural world are made to correspond with his spiritual state—the same causes that produce human parasites producing also the moth, rust, and thief among animals and plants.

Now it has been regarded as an inexplicable mystery how evils come into the world; but the truth is, evils did not come into the world, but are wholly of the world, having been developed here by man's perversion of the good gifts of God through selfishness and sin. It may be said, however, that evils existed here before the coming of man, and that, therefore, man is not responsible for them. And we admit that while the earth was being prepared for the abode of human beings, it was necessarily imperfect, yet that, as in the building of any good house for human habitation, each stage of progressive development in the creation of the earth was a good work, it being precisely fitted for the purpose for which it was designed—that is, for the development therefrom of a stage of still higher advancement (Gen. 1: 12, 18, 21, 25), just as every lower step in a stairway is essential to enable us to reach a higher. While every state of imperfection, to the degree of its imperfection, is an evil state as contrasted with a perfect—being subject to discipline and bondage, as is the human race under the moral law (Gal. 4: 25)—it is yet rightly regarded as good, and as a medium of ascension to a higher state (Gal. 3: 19). Granting, therefore, that before man appeared plants and animals in their struggles for existence warred against each other, and that the fittest survived, we do not admit that this was an evil condition, the

Divine purpose therein being then, as it is now, to develop from an inferior a superior condition of social life. Nor is man, being himself imperfect, necessarily responsible for the evil parasites that now exist, either in his own social life or in that of the lower orders created for his use, any more than is a child for its necessary weakness and ignorance resulting from its immaturity in strength and knowledge; for whether he was originally created a perfect man and became a sinner by transgression, or is only an improved order of animal, God's purpose in him is to develop a perfect being of limitless life and happiness. But if he be unnecessarily imperfect—like a prodigal son, ungrateful for his gifts and opportunities, and spending his substance in riotous living—he is responsible for all evils that exist in his social life, which have resulted from his willful disobedience and profligacy. And it being unquestionably true that we are imperfect, and unnecessarily so—not only not living up to our abilities and opportunities, but also perverting our gifts and wasting our substance in riotous living—the natural law of the survival of the fittest must continue to operate, else the social moth, rust, and thief would survive the more industrious, thrifty, and honest classes. That

is, except we make proper efforts to overcome
evil with good, social degeneration must necessarily ensue with all its incidents of social injustice and suffering.

We should also bear in the mind that parasites are not themselves the original sources of
evils, but only the products thereof, as the diseases of the body are of the perversions of
natural laws upon which health depends. On
the contrary, they are always of use as a matter of discipline, and, like the microbes which
are present in diseased conditions, are scavengers for the removal of useless, offensive, and
decayed substances, howbeit they naturally
propagate themselves, and thus serve to per-
petuate and increase the evils of which they
have themselves been evolved. Thus the microbes which are found present in any diseased
condition, like all evil examples of sin and selfishness, render such diseased condition conta-
gious or infectious by migrating into other
bodies contiguous thereto or within the sphere
of their influence, and developing therein a like
diseased condition. Thus the carpet-moth, for
example, evolved no doubt spontaneously of
the dust and filth, which are the natural accretions of the carpet, may pass into other similar
fabrics, and consume them. All useless things,

as also all useful things put to unnatural uses, naturally begin to rust and decay, and produce the moths which consume our treasures—just as wealth hoarded, or used simply for vain purposes, produces thieves and robbers, who like all other microbes are useful as a discipline and restraint of human cupidity and extravagance.

The law of heredity, whereby the sins of parents are visited upon their children to the third and fourth generations, is a similar illustration how parasites are propagated, and is no doubt useful, just, and merciful, howbeit that children suffer unjustly for the transgressions of their parents,—it being designed to restrain both parents and children from transgression, to give opportunity for repentance and reform (Luke 13: 6-9), and prevent the extermination of the race. For otherwise—if the transgressions of parents were immediately followed by their extermination—there would be no children. Being social beings mutually dependent, we are justly and for our own best interests required to bear each other's burdens as also our own (Gal. 6: 2, 5)—children those of their parents, the strong of the weak, the rich of the poor, the obedient of the disobedient, the wise of the foolish, the thrifty and honest of the profligate and dishonest—that by such discipline we may be impelled to make proper efforts and sacrifices for the reformation and improvement of society.

If, however, a moth, rust, or thief is past redemption—if such be possible—and cannot be made useful when capable of self-support, he should no doubt be exterminated. "The wages of sin is death "—that is, sin is the beginning of death, and if persistent, not repented of, must terminate in death complete. This is in fact the true and practical interpretation of the law of God which we call the survival of the fittest. But as it is impossible for us to determine whether any transgressor be past the possibility of redemption or not, we must strive for the salvation of all. "Vengeance is mine, I will repay, saith the Lord,"—although to this end we are not only permitted but required to enforce the natural and moral laws of God, while at the same time we strive through the charities of the gospel to bring all men to repentance. Nature itself, which is of God and is God, will ultimately exterminate any creature that persistently perverts its gifts to unnatural uses. That is, the law of the survival of the fittest does not exclude the unfit from all participation in God's mercy; for while the wages of sin is death, death does not follow instantly upon transgression (Rom. 5: 20), and where sin abounds grace doth much more abound, so that those who are unfit may become fit to live.

Doubtless the principles whereby all social problems may be rightly solved have been fully and clearly enunciated in the law and the gospel, and all that is essential to the right solution thereof is practically to apply such principles. Yet it seems exceedingly difficult in the present chaotic and complicated conditions of our social life to define in detail the true methods of such application—precisely what legislation and charities are required for the prevention and removal of the Moth, Rust, and Thief—so blinded are we by our selfishness to our own best interests. Like the Pharisees, we do not believe the truth because it is the truth (John 8: 45)—unwilling to accept and apply a practical remedy which requires the sacrifice of our own selfish and temporal interests for the promotion of our unselfish and eternal interests. While we strain at gnats we swallow camels, striving by slight and inefficient efforts to satisfy the requirements of social obligations, and neglecting the weightier matters of justice, mercy, and faith—highly respectable, it may be, according to superficial

and popular standards of religion, and yet pro-
foundly selfish, worldly, and insensible to social
wrongs and oppressions whereby we think we
are made rich and free while others are impoverished and enslaved. Not till we cast out the
beams from our own eyes can we see clearly to
cast out the motes from our brother's eyes—
realizing that we are ourselves moths, rusts,
and thieves so long as we are willing to subsist upon the fruits of other men's labors, and
unwilling to share with them equally—that is,
justly—our own privileges and possessions.

PART I.

THE PROBLEM OF THE MOTH.

WHEN Peter and John were about to enter
at the gate called Beautiful, they were con-
fronted with a great social problem. A crippled and helpless human being was lying there,
who asked of them an alms. He could do
little or nothing in the way of productive industry, and was therefore dependent upon
others for a livelihood—for food, dress, shelter
and all other common necessities and comforts
of life developed by human art of our natural
resources; and to the degree that these were
supplied to him was society impoverished, its
treasures dissipated and its freedom and enjoyment limited. Except as a discipline he never
had been, and did not seem likely ever to become, of any use to society, having been lame
from his mother's womb, but on the contrary
was a tax, a burden, a curse, a pest, living only
by consuming the wealth of others. He was
therefore a moth, feeding at society's table,
reaping where he had not strewn. He was

180

also an unbidden and unwelcome guest, and his presence tolerated only through the natural humanity of men, whereby their natural sympathies were awakened in contemplation of his helpless and suffering condition.

This problem, however, was not new or strange. It was the old problem of poverty and consequent beggary, no doubt originally evolved of man's sinful and corrupted social conditions, one which from remotest times has constantly demanded solution—the more imperatively as the natural intelligence and compassion of society have been developed by religious culture. It is realized in the consciousness of the burdens poverty imposes upon society, and the limitations it places upon the increase and enjoyment of its natural and acquired riches, and consists in the inquiry, how may such burdens and limitation be removed? But while society is in a measure conscious of the existence of this problem, and of the importance and necessity of its solution, its ideas have been and still are indefinite and confused, both as regards the social conditions of which poverty is the natural outcome, and the practical methods by which it may be eliminated.

Barbarians have a very simple and tempora-

rily effective method of dealing with this problem—that is, by either putting to death those
who are not able to take care of themselves, or
suffering them to die by starvation and expos-
ure. Nor is this so inhuman as it may at first
appear, for it is no doubt better for themselves
that such unfortunates should perish at once
than that their lives should be prolonged in a
hopeless condition of suffering.

Among more cultured and Christian people
the usual method is by almsgiving, and by
building hospitals, asylums, or other infirmaries,
which is—of course a good method so far as it
goes, but is simply a temporary expedient, serving only to prolong human suffering and increase
the burdens of society, unless such charities
are accompanied with proper efforts for the
prevention and cure of infirmities.

Now this beggar whom Peter and John encountered was one of a vast variety of moths,
deformed, idiotic or otherwise insane—produced,
not by his own sins, for he was personally, so
far as appears, entirely innocent of all willful
transgressions, but evolved of vicious and perverted social conditions. Deprived thereby of
the natural rights of man, of his natural inheritance of liberty and equality, and yet possessed
of the natural instinct of self-preservation, he

was necessarily a moth. The sins of his parents had been visited upon him,—as doubtless theirs had been upon them,—for it is impossible that he should have been born lame except by the transgression of some natural law. His ancestry may have been so brutalized by enforced ignorance, poverty, and excessive toil, or by hurtful luxuries, criminalities, or dissipations, as to have become incapable of producing healthy offspring. Moths will of course produce moths, and as all men are more or less sinful and selfish, either ·by choice or compulsion, there are probably no perfectly healthy offspring born into the world, and all are in a corresponding degree by birth moths, rusts, and thieves. Nevertheless, if we repent—thereby manifesting the works of God in us (John 9: 1–3)—we may be accounted righteous (2 Thess. 1: 5), and need not perish (Luke 13: 5). No person born a moth need live and die a moth; for as certainly as our infirmities are produced by transgressions of natural, moral, and spiritual laws, so are they healed by obedience thereto. The same law of heredity, whereby social evils are evolved of false habits of life, will, if such habits are corrected, produce a heritage of good. It is folly, therefore, for us to attempt to excuse our transgressions by saying, "Our fathers have eaten sour grapes, and their children's teeth are set on edge " (Ezek. 18 : 2-32). Shall we continue to sin, to oppress the poor, to transmit our infirmities and the curses resulting therefrom to our posterity, because our heritage has been evil ?   God is just, and judges us by our own works, as he also judged our fathers ; and although we suffer and are disciplined for the sins of our fathers, we are condemned only for our own ; and however sorely tempted and oppressed, we are not tempted or oppressed beyond what we are able to bear, if we repent us of our sins and strive to live in obedience to the laws of God (1 Cor. 10 : 13).

It is therefore our imperative duty and our highest privilege to strive to prevent and cure the social evils with which we are afflicted, and for which we are responsible.   Indeed, unless we do make this effort our redemption is impossible, and we shall be justly condemned, not only for our own transgressions, but also for the sins of our parents.

To this variety of moths belongs also that which is produced, not directly by birth, as this beggar was, but by the social circumstances and conditions into which it is born, which tempt and even compel men to lead unnatural lives—born into poverty and ceaseless toil, brought up in ignorance and brutality, and with little or no opportunities for the culture and improvement of their natural rights and endowments. Or they may have been—and such examples are not infrequent—born in affluence and afterward reduced to poverty, in which case, not having been trained in habits of industry, they are incapable of earning a livelihood, and become most pitiable objects of charity. Such persons may have led honest lives, but through stress of excessive toil or misfortune have become so physically, mentally, or spiritually debilitated that they are incapable of self-support, and compelled to become beggars and tramps. Surely there must be something radically wrong in our social polity that compels human beings to be born beggars, or permits any who are unwilling to steal and are able and willing to work to become a public charge. Nor is it difficult to discover and right such wrong, if we do not permit ourselves to be blinded by selfishness, or so corrupted thereby that we have become indifferent thereto, and unwilling to make any proper efforts and sacrifices to right it.

Another variety is that which is produced neither by its own inherited disabilities nor by such vitiated conditions of birth as compel it to lead an unnatural life, but by the necessities of society incurred by the disabilities of other members thereof. If one member is disabled another must take care of him, and to the degree the latter is thus occupied, he is rendered incapable of productive industries, and must be supported by others. It may seem unkind and unjust to call him a moth, his work being necessary and charitable, yet he is no more innocent of offence than this beggar was, and as he is by his calling rendered incapable of contributing to the wealth of society, he becomes a tax upon its recourses. Every hospital, asylum, or infirmary requires an army of officials, nurses, physicians, cooks, and scavengers, all of whom consume what others produce, and contribute nothing to their own support; and though very useful, as a discipline of our sin and selfishness, in ministering to the unfortunate necessities of society developed therefrom, they are yet parasites, evolved of social suffering, sin, and selfishness.

But there are many other varieties, not quite so innocent, yet guiltless of any intentional offence, who produce such things as are supposed to be needed and are sanctioned by the civil laws, but are either useless or positively harmful. Thus when Paul was preaching at Eph-

esus he encountered this variety in the person
of the silversmith Demetrius (Acts 19: 24–27)
and others of his craft, who built silver shrines
for "The Great Goddess Diana," whom the
people worshipped, believing her to be a
daughter of Jupiter, and that her image had
dropped down from heaven upon the site of the
great temple subsequently erected to her
honor. This faith was of course a popular delusion, but as "all Asia and the world" believed it, the manufacture of her silver shrines
was considered a highly honorable calling,
though in fact highly detrimental to the best
interests of the people, tending, as it did, to
impoverish them by limiting the production of
actual necessities, and wasting the real treasures of life—although it tended to the concen-
tration of wealth at Ephesus, and gave employment to many workmen. All concentrations of wealth, whether in places or persons,
can only result in the impoverishment of other
places and persons, except it be held by its
possessors for the use and enrichment of all;
and it is of no benefit to society that any
workmen should find employment in the production of useless things, but on the contrary,
by thus limiting the number of useful laborers,

its capacity for the acquirement of real riches is correspondingly limited.

All superstitions are destructive of real riches, whether material or spiritual, and all persons who derive a livelihood therefrom, are social moths. And no doubt there are very many superstitions in the churches, some of which are as great and harmful as that which obtained at Ephesus, and which in like manner by concentrating wealth and giving employment to many craftsmen, delude the masses into the belief that they represent the true culture of religion and the well-being of society. Like the ancient Athenians many congregations nominally Christian worship unknown gods, are too superstitious (Acts 17 : 22, 23), and as a natural and inevitable sequence thereof breed and feed a great many moths. Their theological schools, so called, instead of teaching the Fatherhood of God and the Brotherhood of Man—which is the one and only true religion—are mostly devoted to a sectarian idolatry directly opposed to the spirit of unity in the gospel, and instead of graduating young men into the ministry of Christ turn out a multitude of clerical parasites, who obtain a livelihood by catering to the eccentricities, bigotries, and prejudices of the sects they represent, or to the worldly pride

and vanity of the people who patronize them—
flatterers, toadies, sycophants, puppets, alive it
may be to the letter of the gospel, but dead to
its spirit; "having a form of godliness but
denying the power thereof": leading "captive
silly women"; "ever learning and never able
to come to the knowledge of the truth" (2
Tim. 3: 5–7). "Nevertheless the foundation
of God standeth sure, having this seal, The
Lord knoweth them that are his" (2 Tim. 2:
19); and although Christ be preached in pretence or in envy and strife, he is yet preached,
and therein we may rejoice (Phil. 1: 15–18);
for the gospel is a social leaven (Matt. 13: 33),
and must produce fermentation until the im-
purities of the church are eliminated, and the
whole lump is leavened. No doubt these
clerical moths, being blinded to the real mission of the Christ, and moreover being compelled to seek their bread from the world, are
guiltless of intentional offence, and really believe they are doing God's service. Nor are we
to believe that the ministry as a whole are insensible to their real mission; for no doubt
most ministers of the Church, were they re-
lieved from the stress of worldly necessities
whereby the flesh is made weak, would speak
boldly in condemnation of all worldly pride.

vanity, selfishness, and injustice, and in defence
of the rights and liberties of oppressed and
suffering humanity. As in every " great house
there are not only vessels of gold and silver,
but also of wood and of earth, and some to
honor and some to dishonor " (2 Tim. 2: 20),
so even in a corrupted church there are some
true prophets and priests of God, and some intent only on the professional and perfunctory
discharge of such religious obligations as are
imposed upon them by the sects they represent.

Besides its clerical moths, there are many
other parasites evolved and developed of the
Church corrupted through worldly influences,
who consume and waste its treasures—beggars
who subsist upon the misplaced alms it bestows
upon the poor; laymen who avail themselves
of its popularity to promote their personal,
worldly, and selfish interests; laywomen intent
only on getting into good society so called, devoted to fanciful forms of worship that involve
great and useless expense, and to " outward
adorning " rather than to the incorruptible
treasures of the heart (1 Pet. 3: 3, 4).

Even the charities of the church are largely
perverted, being consumed and wasted by
moths—all, in fact, that are not accompanied
by practical efforts to prevent and cure infirmi-

ties. And charity thus perverted is no longer
charity, serving only to produce and develop
the evils it is intended to alleviate. Charity,
the love of God and Man, being the end of the
law for righteousness (1 Tim. 1 : 5), all gifts
and sacrifices are wasted that are not devoted
to this end; and all who make such gifts or
sacrifices, as also all who are occupied in their
distribution, are moths, not only useless to society but destroyers of its treasures.   To
merely mitigate and tide over present distresses
is straining at gnats, seeking to excuse ourselves for the social evils for which we are ourselves guilty, which have produced such distresses, and for our neglects of the weightier
matters of the gospel whereby equal rights and
privileges may be bestowed upon all men.   If
by our charities we do not seek to make the
objects thereof as free and equal as ourselves,
they are not only wasted, but encourage and
develop beggary.   Moreover, if we bestow
alms, not for the salvation of the poor, but for
our own personal salvation—only with the idea
that with such gifts we purchase for ourselves
salvation—our motive is simply selfish and
purchases our own damnation ; for it multiplies
beggars and the consequent burdens and curses
inflicted upon us.   We may even give all our

goods to feed the poor, or our bodies to be burned (1 Cor. 13: 3), and neither receive for ourselves nor bestow any profit upon others, because our motive is vainglorious.

So also, through denominationalism and lack of unity and brotherly love in the church, our missionary offerings designed for the conversion of the heathen are largely dissipated, and the missionaries we employ converted into clerical moths. As the sole purpose of the gospel of the Christ is the practical culture of the love of God and of our fellow-men—which is unity with God and with each other—it is manifestly impossible to convert men to the Christian faith except there be unity in the churches. Sectarianism is itself disunity, and is directly opposed to the spirit of this gospel; for so long as we are ourselves divided it is but hypocrisy to preach the Fatherhood of God and the Brotherhood of Man. And however great our zeal, though we compass sea and land to make one proselyte (Matt. 23: 15), we cannot, being ourselves mere parasites of the Church and lacking the Spirit of our Master, clothe our converts in his "wedding garment."

But while this parasite abounds in the churches of our day, subsisting upon its dissipating and dissipated charities, its worldly vanities, bigotries, and superstitions that have crept in unawares (Gal. 2: 4; 3: 1; Jude 4), it yet much more abounds in the world—being found in almost every profession and calling—not including common beggars and tramps. These are notoriously political moths who feed upon the loaves and fishes of office ; and, although they may represent the will of the people, are but blind leaders of the blind, doing nothing for the improvement and well-being of society, itself corrupt through ignorance, lust, selfishness, and sin, and insensible to its own best interests. There is no greater error than to suppose it to be the duty of any person elected to office to represent his constituency by catering to their partisan or selfish interests; for such representation is not for the true interests of the people but against them. Those only are capable of representing the people who apprehend what the best interests of the people are as determined by the natural, moral, and spiritual laws of God. As a true father represents the best interests of his children, not by humoring their whims, follies, caprices, and undisciplined passions, but by seeking to promote their real and permanent welfare, so should every executive officer, legislator, or judge seek to perceive and do, not what the people in their

blindness may desire, but what serves best to promote their real and enduring prosperity. This is
the highest statesmanship, the highest political
wisdom, a ruler of the people can possess,—that
which, like the gift God bestowed upon Solo-
mon, is the ability and desire to discern and
judge between good and bad (1 Kings 3: 9).
All other political wisdom is but foolishness
with God.

Of like character are lawyers who pervert
their otherwise noble profession into a system
of pettifoggery.. And all lawyers who obtain a
living by low cunning and trickery are petti-
foggers and evil parasites—intent only upon
securing large fees, and instead of cultivating,
teaching, and enforcing the principles of law
and vindicating the rights and liberties of men
as their profession requires, foment strife and
defend and justify iniquity.—Of the same kind
also are quack doctors of medicine,—and all
doctors are quacks, however otherwise learned,
whose motive is chiefly selfish—the purpose
and desire of personal gain through the physical
and mental infirmities and misfortunes of their
fellow-men,—who think they have discharged
their whole duty when they have administered
poisonous drugs as antidotes for the temporary
relief of their patients, while they do nothing

for the permanent cure and prevention of diseases and infirmities; whereas it is quite as much the duty of the physician of the body to study, teach, and preach the fundamental principles upon which physical health depends, as it is for the physician of the soul to inculcate the principles of moral and spiritual laws essential to its present and eternal welfare.

The like is also true of literateurs, artists, and musicians, whose ideals and realizations of their otherwise useful callings contribute little or nothing to the true culture of society, serving only to satisfy morbid cravings for entertainment, and whose merits are estimated only by their commercial value. Also of manufacturers, merchants, craftsmen, laborers, so far as they produce, distribute, construct, or handle needless or harmful luxuries of dress, food, drink, shelter or any other thing, the desire or necessity of which is evolved and developed of corrupt and unnatural social conditions. Nor are educators, students, journalists, who teach, study, or disseminate such knowledge, wisdom, or information as is foolishness with God, or positively corrupting and harmful in our social life, other than evil parasites.

With such a vast and varied multitude of people who are supported by society, but who

contribute little or nothing to its wealth, we
cannot wonder there should be so much poverty
and distress in the world.   There are enough
and more than enough riches consumed by
moths to supply all the real necessities and
comforts of the poor, and if this destructive
element were eliminated, as it easily might be,
and converted into useful and productive industry, social suffering and oppression would
be correspondingly alleviated.

PART II.

AKIN to the Moth, but varying therefrom in species, there is another social parasite whom the Christ designated as the Rust. As in the physical so in the spiritual world—that is, as in those of Substance, so also in the evolutions and developments of the principles of Nature and Art—rust represents a process of disintegration, whether by slow burning or rapid conflagration. Its presence in society, tending to decompose and weaken the religious bond that binds men to God and to each other, is certain evidence of social degeneration and decay, and unless removed is· the sure harbinger of ultimate and complete disintegration. Its first symptom is usually a foul accretion at the surface, which, if not wiped away, burns deeper and deeper into the system till the whole organism is dissipated.

Although this beggar is properly classified as a moth, a social parasite distinct in species from the Rust, he was yet of the same genus or

197

kind, as all parasites are, illustrating, as he did, in his whole physical, mental, and spiritual organism the process of suppression, waste, and dissipation of his faculties. By his one infirmity the natural endowments and activities of a human being had been repressed in him, and were in a state of rust and decay, it being a natural law that any organism not used for the purpose for which it was designed shall be destroyed. Yet he differed from the Rust, not having by his own act incurred his disability, and not unwilling to help himself.

As Rust is dissipation, that of society is represented in all dissipated members thereof, who waste its treasures, either by indisposition to use and improve them, or by perverting them to unnatural uses ; and is like the Moth of many varieties—physical, mental, and spiritual. Nor are these varieties limited to any particular classes,—rich or poor, learned or unlearned, religious or irreligious—all being more or less dissipated in body, mind, and spirit, through selfishness, and may all be described as the intemperate elements of our social life—the gluttonous and drunken, the profligate and licentious, the prodigal and extravagant, the indolent and thriftless.

Manifestly to the degree that such rust exists is society impoverished, and there is presented therein a great social problem, the solution of which is absolutely essential to the stability and progress of our race. While dissipation exists, and we derive a fictitious and harmful pleasure therein, even riches become a curse, a source of poverty and distress, and the more the one is increased, so much the more is the other also. Rust could not exist if there were nothing for it to feed upon ; and as wealth unused or perverted to evil purposes induces rust, the greater the apparent wealth of a corrupt community, the greater also will be its rust and a corresponding lack of freedom, equity, and brotherhood. What then ? Must we be poor in order to be temperate ? Must we have nothing that there may be no opportunity for rust ? No doubt this is natural law—that perverted wealth shall develop poverty ; that to the degree we misuse our good gifts are they taken from us,— but if we use them for the purpose for which they are designed, which is to minister to our necessities, they will increase· as our necessities increase through the development of our capacities for enjoyment by true culture and refinement. Our necessities are the precise measure of our real wealth, being all things essential to our sustenance, growth, comfort, and enjoyment. Thus proper food and drink, being the mediums of physical life and its preservation, are real treasures. Hence by nature we hunger and thirst, and from the satisfaction of such cravings we naturally derive substantial blessings; but if through a vitiated art we unduly stimulate and pamper our appetites that we may unnaturally increase and prolong enjoyments, we become gluttonous and drunken, weaken and decrease our capacities for enjoyment, and waste and destroy our treasures.

Temperance is moderation; and moderation is the economical adjustment of our desires and uses to our actual necessities (Phil. 4: 5). If therefore we desire or use more or less than we need, we are intemperate—there being in the one case loss through excess, and in the other through deprivation,—and in either case our faculties for enjoyment are impaired and our treasures wasted. That is, superfluity and want, gluttony and starvation, are equally intemperate, and produce rust and decay.

As the necessities of society increase with the increase of its culture in its ability to possess and enjoy, and as society is one organic whole, it is plain that such necessities must be experienced alike by all members thereof; and to the degree that there is inequality—some having more than enough to supply their necessities, and others less—there will be intemperance. That is, social moderation—an absence of excess either in the use or disuse of necessities— is impossible without social equality. In fact moderation is equality—a just equilibrium of necessities among all members, and in opportunities of supplying such necessities. Hence, if the rich, having more than they need, waste their substance in riotous living—in indolence, luxury, and extravagance,—society is rusted and in a condition of decay to the degree of such waste (Jas. 5: 1–3); and the same is true to the degree that the poor are deprived of what is needful to their well-being and increased capacities for acquirement and happiness. Extremes are always unsocial, and meet in the production of the same social rust—extremes of wealth with those of poverty, of gluttony with starvation, of extravagance in dress with rags and nakedness, of culture with brutality, of pleasure with pain, of charity with beggary, of industrial devotion with avarice, and even of religious zeal with spiritual apathy. Thus the source of Rust like that of other parasites is traced to an unsocial and therefore an unnatural condition of society; and such condition is itself the result of selfishness whereby the interests of individuals and classes are separated from, and made antagonistic to, each other. If, therefore, we would promote temperance we should promote social equality. And if we would promote equality we should promote temperance; for neither can exist without the other.

To be sure, society cannot be temperate so long as individuals are intemperate; but it is equally true that individuals cannot be temperate so long as society is intemperate. No doubt society and the individuals who compose it are mutually responsible for their existing social conditions, yet society is primarily responsible, inasmuch as it is empowered to compel obedience to the laws of God; and although it cannot be perfect except to the degree that such laws are fulfilled in love—that is voluntarily—by its individual members, it can improve to the degree that it enforces such laws, the law being a schoolmaster to bring us to Christ (Gal. 3: 24). So long, therefore, as society not only tolerates inequalities in its members, but also enforces them, it is impossible to solve the problem of social rust. Thus while the poor man is compelled to live in a condition of unnatural repression in the use, culture, and enjoyment of the natural gifts God has bestowed upon all men alike—to toil constantly, not only for his own daily bread, clothing and shelter, but also to supply the rich with superfluities, and enable them to live in idleness, luxury, and pleasure,—all legislation to enforce temperate and economical living is either hypocritical, or a mere straining at gnats. Not till all classes are given equal opportunities for physical, mental, and spiritual culture, and each is compelled to contribute according to his abilities equally to the productive industries of society, —to its food, drink, clothing, shelter, care, instruction, and general improvement, can the evils of intemperance and social rust be eliminated.

Now one of the greatest obstacles to the promotion of temperance is the limited conception of its meaning in the popular mind. Thus, if one abstains from the use of strong drinks, he is regarded as sufficiently temperate, whereas total abstinence from any good thing, though often necessary as a discipline in our perverted social condition, is not temperance, but on the contrary intemperance, God permitting—nay even requiring us as essential to our welfare— to use in moderation all things he has bestowed

upon us, as also all things we can lawfully develop and acquire from our natural resources
(1 Cor. 6 : 12–20 ; 10 : 23–31 ; Col. 2 : 16–20).
Intemperance is always excess (Eph. 5 : 18 ;
1 Pet. 4 : 3, 4) ; and any excess is always intemperance—excess in what is otherwise good.

Now as the love of money is a root of all evil,
and notably among people professedly Christian, from such love are evolved and developed
all evil parasites, especially the Rust. Doubtless the excessive, enslaving, and almost exclusive devotion of our age to what is called business is its greatest dissipation, tempting and
even compelling, as it does, most men to lead
unnatural lives—to devote their whole time
and strength to the accumulation and hoarding
of treasures on earth, "where moth and rust
doth corrupt and where thieves break through
and steal," or simply to save themselves from
penury and starvation. In this way selfishness
is cultured and even made a necessity, while
our higher emotional, intellectual, moral, and
religious faculties are repressed and rusted. In
fact, every infirmity and social evil, all waste,
dissipation, and thievery, may be traced to this
one root of all evil, the love of money ; and as
this love is more cultured and stimulated in
our day than it has ever been before, more

and worse varieties of evil parasites have been produced. Most social interests have become thereby venal—whether political, industrial, educational, or religious,—and their value estimated by the money that is in them. Little else is regarded of any utility or profit, whether of occupations, honors, rewards or aspirations. In short, Mammon has come to be worshipped as the one only living and true God. Naturally, either compelled by the stress of poverty, or incited thereto by the greed of gain, our energies have become chiefly devoted to the development of earthly riches, and as a natural sequence thereof—it being impossible to transfer such riches to the next life, while our spiritual nature has been repressed by our exclusive devotion to them—there has been a corresponding development of social rust. Human art has been perverted and stimulated to the utmost, not only to acquire earthly riches, but also to devise means for the sensual enjoyment thereof in foods, drinks, dresses, houses, decorations, and entertainments.

Now it should be manifest that the true church—that social condition in which there is unity of interests, purposes, and aspirations, and, through the love of God and of each other, an equality of opportunities and privileges con-

ferred—represents the true and only social condition in which neither moth nor rust doth corrupt, nor thieves break through and steal. But
it is as impossible that there should be a true
church in which inequality and consequent intemperance, waste, and dissipation are tolerated, as that there should be a kingdom of
Heaven in which evil parasites exist (1 Cor.
6: 9, 10; Gal. 5: 21).—although while yet
imperfect, as it must necessarily be in a sinful
world, its faith is counted unto it for righteousness, if it strive to practically realize its true
ideal. To the degree, therefore, that the church
has itself become degenerate and rusted, and
not only tolerates unjust social inequalities, but
evolves, develops, and propagates dissipation or
any other evil parasite, is its power of redemption impaired. And that it is greatly rusted
cannot be doubted—full of worldly inequalities
and excesses:—wisdom that is foolishness with
God (1 Cor. 3: 19),—fashions that pass away
(1 Cor. 7: 31),—friendships of the world that
are enmity with God (Jas. 4: 4),—lying vanities (Jonah 2: 8; Acts 14: 15),—cares of this
world and deceitfulness of riches (Matt. 13: 22),
—lusts of the flesh and of the eyes, and the
pride of life (1 John 1: 16),—and all other dissipations typified in the Scarlet Woman (Rev.

17: 1-6), and in the Babylon of a perverted
and corrupted social life (Rev. 18: 2, 3).

It is, of course, easy enough to form a congregation, but to constitute a church of Christ
such congregation must have an eye single to
his service (Matt. 6: 22, 23; Acts 2: 46).. Its
spirit must be his spirit (Rom. 8: 9), its purpose his purpose (Eph. 3: 10, 11), its works his
works (John 4: 34; Jas. 1: 25; Rev. 2: 26).
Otherwise, though it be called a church, it is of
the world, of the earth earthy. In short, if it
represent anything more or less in its teachings
and worship than the mission of the Christ, it is
not his congregation. All else cometh of evil
(Matt. 5: 37).

While in the true church there is growth in
all useful things—in knowledge, strength, life,
and enjoyment—which is the increase of faith,
patience, hope, and charity, all other increase is
but evidence of dissipation—the foul accretions
of rust and mould, or the fungous growths
which, though often pretty, are evolved of disease and decay. Such foul accretions are ecclesiasticisms, and all ecclesiasticisms are foul
accretions, coming of evil—all conventional and
professional titles whereby personal and exclusive distinctions, prerogatives, emoluments, privileges, and powers are conferred (Job 32: 21,

22; Matt. 23: 5–10). None of the apostles assumed any such titles, but in obedience to their Master were content to be called his servants—the very highest title that can be conferred upon men (Matt. 23: 11, 12). In fact the idea of the Church, which is Christ's Body, has become so obscured in ecclesiasticisms, that it is difficult to discern therein its real character and mission. There is excess of ritual in place of worship; churchiness in place of churchliness; much praying to be seen of men, mere Phariseeism and lip service (Matt. 6: 5; 15: 8), asking God to do for us what we can and should do for ourselves (Ex. 14, 15; Phil. 2: 12), which is but weariness to him (Isa. 1: 14, 15)—in place of personal effort and sacrifice, seeking to know and do our duty to God and man, and the culture of true desires and aspirations. Of like character are sacramentalisms, whereby sacred rites, ordained in the Church by the Christ and his apostles as tokens of his covenants and promises, are made ·magic arts and forms of superstition and fetichism; sacerdotalisms in place of preaching and prophecy; morbid pietisms in place of practical, spiritual, and manly culture; childish pipings for others to dance and mournings for others to lament (Matt. 11: 16, 17) in place of manly exhortations, moral courage, and earnest and practical sympathy with wronged and suffering humanity; speculative creeds and dogmas of man's appointment in place of the plain and simple principles of faith in Jesus Christ (Isa. 35: 8; John 7: 17); sectarianisms, built on such man-made creeds (Matt. 15: 9; Eph. 4: 14), in place of unity and brotherly love; austerity in place of cheerfulness (Zech. 8: 19; Matt. 6: 16–18); mystery, soothsaying, sorcery, and magic in place of enlightenment, spiritual culture and power, and genuine miracles (Isa. 2: 6–9; Acts 8: 11; Rev. 17: 5; 18: 23)—all mystery, darkness, and superstition having been dispelled in the coming of the Christ (Matt. 10: 26; 13: 11; Acts 17: 22, 23; 1 Cor. 4: 5; Eph. 3: 9); excess of music and decoration in place of heartfelt praise (Ps. 138: 1, 2), the refinements of divine art, and the ineffable beauty of holiness (Ps. 29: 2), which are found only in simplicity (Matt. 6: 28, 29; 2 Cor. 11: 3); sentimentalism and sensationalism in place of study and teaching and the practical culture of knowledge in the Way, Truth, and Life of God (Eccl. 7: 25; Luke 8: 15; 2 Tim. 2: 15, 16); making clean the outside of the cup while within it is full of extortion and excess; deferring wholly to the next life the realization of the hope and promise of the gospel in order to avoid the necessary sacrifice and discipline of the present life (Isa. 49: 7, 8; 2 Cor. 6: 2; Jas. 2: 16); giving silver and gold instead of taking the poor by the hand, setting them on their feet and making them equal with ourselves in opportunities (Acts 3: 4-8)—as if we thought the gifts of God could be purchased with money (Acts 8: 28).

All these are of a sinful and selfish world, whose friendship is enmity with God,—deviations from the straight and narrow way—neither forgetting the things which are behind, nor pressing forward unto the things which are before, but turning again to the enslaving and beggarly rudiments of the world (Gal. 4: 3-9; Col. 2: 8, 20), to its idolatries, superstitions, bigotries, pomps, and vanities. There is but one mark set before the church,—the prize of the high calling of God in Christ Jesus, the Perfect Manhood, "the measure of the stature of the fullness of Christ," in which only can be realized a social condition of perfect liberty (John 8: 36), equality (Rom. 8: 14-17), and fraternity (Mark 3: 35). All ecclesiasticisms, and indeed all other isms, are excesses and symptoms of dissipation and rust,—at the best unessential, and therefore extravagances, gluttonies, adulteries, and riotous living. Wherefore, as the true Church of Christ represents the one and only true system of sociology, it is plain that this great problem of the Rust can be practically solved only by the regeneration, reformation, and renovation of its present congregations, whereby all dissipations, extravagances, and unessential things may be suppressed and eliminated, and the true economies and increase of faith, hope, and charity be cultured through the love of God and Man. When it is itself redeemed from its degeneracies it may redeem the world, but not otherwise.

PART III.

THE PROBLEM OF THE THIEF.

As charity is the crowning virtue, so is thievery the crowning vice—it being, either in letter or spirit, the transgression of every social law ; and as the God of love is the giver of all good gifts, so is Satan the thief and destroyer (Mark 4: 15; 1 Pet. 5: 8). Hence, to the degree we are charitable and do unto others as we would they should do unto us, are we honest and godly ; and to the degree we are selfish and rob and oppress each other are we dishonest and satanic.

Now if, as we have shown, most evil parasites are developed in society by its own transgressions or perversions of the natural and moral laws of God, it is responsible for the existence of the thief so far as it lacks in disposition and effort to reform itself. It is, in fact, impossible there should be any occasion for thievery, if all members or classes could possess all that justly belongs to them, and were given equal opportunities for honestly acquiring all things essential to their well-being; and if we would clearly understand this social problem, and practically apply our knowledge to its solution, we must become conscious and repent us of our sin and selfishness, whereby others are deprived of equal rights and opportunities with ourselves, and tempted and often in a measure compelled to steal in order to obtain a livelihood. Simply punishing the offender by fine and imprisonment will avail little so long as we ourselves, whether consciously or unconsciously, are guilty of the like offence (Matt. 18: 7). While we may and should punish thieves if we ourselves are guiltless of thievery, it but involves us in a like offence to attempt to cast motes out of our brother's eyes when there are beams in our own eyes. And that we are guilty is self-evident if we willingly permit the necessity of stealing, or the temptation thereto, to exist through our own cupidity, injustice, and oppression.

As like produces like—and nothing could exist wholly unlike that which produced it—society must be like the thief it has evolved, and in its organic unity, in the established relations of its members and classes to each other, be in conflict with the principles of true religion—of natural, moral, and spiritual laws

(Jer. 22 : 13). Its motives and methods must
be the motives and methods of the thief; and
as the thief is selfish, and takes without right
or leave that which belongs to another, so must
the various members and classes of society be
also selfish and transgressors upon each other's
rights. The only difference is that society
does this openly by a process of thievery called
civil law (Isa. 10 : 1), and the common thief
stealthily in violation thereof. And yet we
have no right to say that, because other persons hold greater possessions than we under the
civil law, they are thieves; for such persons
may be temperate, and saving, while we may
be, or our progenitors from whom we may have
inherited our poverty may have been, intemperate and wasteful.

Civil laws, so far as they are in harmony
with the laws of God both in letter and spirit,
are practically God's laws, but if administered
only in the letter, or in the spirit of selfishness, are unequal, and are simply devices of
Satan for the enslavement of men. The real
motive of all God's laws is charity, and in the
spirit of love only can they be fulfilled; and
the same should be true also of all civil laws,
for otherwise they become only mediums of
avarice and oppression. Hence, if under the

protection of the civil laws, any member or class of society acquires wealth and holds it selfishly and exclusively to his own use, the same is a thief and robber (Rom. 2 : 21); and in like manner any member who, under the law—which when it says, "thou shalt not steal," means also that thou shalt earn thine own living—is poor through his own dissipation and thriftlessness (Hag. 1 : 6, 15), also a thief and robber. Civil laws can be brought into harmony with divine laws only when they do not permit any man to be selfishly rich or needlessly poor; and when this is accomplished this problem of the thief is solved, so far as by law it can be solved—not fully in the spirit, but in the letter. Such solution, however,—that is, by compulsory equality—is possible only to the degree that society is leavened with the spirit of the gospel; for so long as individuals and classes are indisposed to do unto others as they would that others should do unto them, are they indisposed to enforce the laws. In other words, thieves cannot be entrusted to enforce the laws they themselves violate either in the letter or in the spirit.

Assuming, therefore, that this problem cannot be practically and finally solved except through the influence of Christian principles,

it is self-evident that the congregations of the
church must, if they would save the world
or themselves, present examples of voluntary
honesty and social equality—that is, social
equity, which is true equality—in themselves,
and, to the utmost of their power and influence
in the world, by the enforcement therein of the
natural and moral laws of God, strive to repress
all thievery. For if the church cannot solve
this problem in itself, it surely cannot solve it
in the world.

Now while we would not say that the church
of our day has become a den of thieves—it
representing, as it doubtless does, the best
moral and religious culture society has attained
since the Apostolic Church became corrupted—
its congregations are yet very far from realizing
in themselves and presenting to the world such
examples of social equity as existed in the
Divine Original.

While in so many words it is instructed that
it cannot serve two masters, for either it will
hate the one and love the other, or else it will
hold to the one and despise the other, it yet
attempts to serve both God and Mammon (Matt.
6: 24)—forgetful that friendship to the world
is enmity to God; not making the mammon of
unrighteousness friendly to itself, but itself

friendly to the mammon of unrighteousness. Indeed it is impossible to estimate to how great an extent its congregations are robbed by systematic trickeries and impositions practiced upon them through their vanities, ignorances, and superstitions, whereby they are made to believe they are purchasing salvation with money, and by devoting their time to the observance of worse than useless ecclesiasticisms. Moreover, in its social polities, instead of presenting an example for the world to follow, the church follows the ways of the world, and presents in itself similar social inequalities and inequities.

In the church as in the world the love of money is a root of all evils,—of thievery as well as of rust and beggary,—for all selfish inequalities are thievery; and so far as there is this love in the congregation is there thievery in spirit. Nor can this spirit be effaced so long as clergymen's salaries are regarded as pay for their labors rather than voluntary contributions to their necessities (Phil. 4: 16-19); for anyone who receives pay or reward beyond his actual necessities for the service he justly owes as a social being to his neighbors is necessarily avaricious (Ezek. 34: 2-10); and if any be unwilling to share his salary equally with his brethren according to their needs, he is in spirit selfish and thievish. Each, if he would be as his Master (Luke 6 : 40), must be content with his penny, even though he have borne the burden and heat of the day (Matt. 20 : 1-15). And what is true of the ministry in relation to their salaries is true of the laity in relation to their incomes (Luke 18 : 22; Acts 4: 34, 35; Rom. 12 : 13; Eph. 4: 28; 1 Tim. 6 : 17, 18), for one who is unwilling to give as he receives is also selfish and thievish (Ezek. 34 : 17-31), blind to his own best interests, and cannot enter into the Kingdom of God.

So also any member of the church, whether clerical or lay, who receives and accepts any contribution or income for useless labors, bestowed through the misfortunes, ignorances, superstitions or bigotries of others, is not only a moth and rust, but also a thief. Nothing whatever deserves or can justly claim any reward in this life or the next that is not, like virtue, its own reward, and conducive to the eternal and social well-being of men. All ministrations and moneys, therefore, that are not contributed to real necessities of life and happiness are wasted; and being selfishly procured through the ignorant credulity of the people, are taken by stealth and stolen. To receive a salary, for example, for pastoral work, and yet devote one's time and the contributions of ignorant and deluded people to ministrations in rusty ecclesiasticisms and dogmatic and sectarian bigotries, or to any other object than the culture of love and obedience to God the Father, and unity and brotherhood in God the Son, is in the highest degree hypocritical and dishonest (Ezek. 13: 1–23).

Although the Thief is of many varieties, as many and varied as our treasures, he may be divided into two general classes—that which transgresses the law in the letter, and that which transgresses it in the spirit—the disreputable and criminal, and the quasi respectable and speciously honest elements of society. Of the former class—all guilty of the familiar crimes of larceny, burglary, robbery, false pretences, embezzlement, forgery, bribery, adultery, usury, malicious mischief, disorderly conduct, conspiracy, rioting, assault, arson, rape, voluntary or involuntary manslaughter, slander, or any other wileful and wilful trangressions of the letter of the law—it is not necessary to write in detail, but to the latter, of which society is little conscious, but of which the criminal classes have been primarily evolved, we should give careful study and reflection. This includes all persons whose ruling motive is selfishness, howbeit they may be strict observers of the letter of the law.

Indeed all persons to the degree of their self-ishness are dishonest, neither loving God nor their neighbor, and not unwilling to appropriate to their own exclusive use what justly belongs to others. As taught in the gospel of the Christ, the law, except it be fulfilled in love, is simply a system of bondage, whereby the strong and rich are enabled to oppress the weak and the poor (Jas. 2: 6-16), or the dissipated and needlessly ignorant or indigent become burdens upon the intelligent, thrifty, and temperate. To be selfishly learned or illiterate, rich or poor, temperate or intemperate, religious or irreli-gious, is thievery—indisposition or neglect to pay what each as a social being owes to God and his fellow-men.

Selfishness is manifestly directly opposed to love, and as love is the source of life, selfishness is inimical thereto—limiting and wasting, as it does, the possessions and enjoyments of all riches whereby life is developed and distributed. And as for one to deprive another of the opportunity of acquiring riches is equivalent to stealing them from him, selfishness is thievery. But love itself may be so limited and perverted as

to become selfish. Pure love is a sincere desire to promote the well-being of all men,
whether friends or enemies (Matt. 5: 43-47).
Hence, to love those who only love us, or those
only of our own family or class, whether rich
or poor, employers or employees, being partial,
is selfish and thievish in spirit. The gospel
teaches that the Christ died for all men (2 Cor.
5: 14, 15), and that, while all were dead in
trespasses and sins, he came that we might
have life, and might have it more abundantly
(John 10: 10),—not as the thief "but for to
steal, to kill, and to destroy," not as the princes
of this world to exercise temporal dominion in
their own selfish interests, but as the minister
and servant of men—even "to give his life as a
ransom for many" (Matt. 20: 25-28). Such
pure, unselfish love, therefore, being Christ's
motive, it is manifestly true that no person can
have a true and saving faith in him, except to
the degree he is ruled by a like motive. Without it there is in fact no conception or practical
experience of God's grace—a word expressive
of pure unselfishness, of such gratitude for and
responsiveness to, good gifts, and such appre-
ciation of privileges and opportunities conferred
upon us, as impels us to return love and kindness for love and kindness shown us, and to im-

prove our gifts, opportunities, and privileges
thus conferred by striving to confer like gifts,
opportunities, and privileges upon others who
need them. In fact, lack of Christian grace in
any member of the Church—an indisposition to
give as he has received—renders him a hypocrite and thief; for there is no worse dishonesty
and thievery in spirit than ingratitude—the
selfishly appropriating to our exclusive use that
which has been bestowed upon us, without
making any return. And yet this sacred and
most practical word—grace—has largely become a merely professional term or shibboleth
or fetich in the churches—rolled under the
tongue as a sweet morsel by priests and congregations besotted in worldliness, superstition,
and pharisaical self-righteousness, and regarded
as expressive of a magical infusion of holiness!
—thus bedaubing themselves with untempered
mortar (Ezek. 22: 28).

All worldly pride and vanity, being necessarily selfish and destitute of grace, render us
thieves in spirit (Ps. 101: 5; Prov. 6: 17; 1
John 2: 16, 17); and the same is true of envy
(Prov. 3: 31; 14: 30; 1 Cor. 13: 4; Jas. 4:
5, 6). Pride and envy, the one despising the
poor, and the other hating the rich, are partners
in thievery, persecuting and robbing each other.

Hence aristocratism, pride of power or station, contemptuous of men of low estate, unsympathetic with poverty and distress, and jealous and repressive of all efforts or aspirations on the part of the masses to improve their social conditions—as also democratism, demagogy, craftily pandering to popular prejudices, ignorances, superstitions, and vulgarities in order to promote selfish ends, affecting and assuming equality with superior merit, or seeking to exalt itself by disparaging and abasing others—being in spirit persecuting, is unchristian and dishonest (Prov. 21: 4, 24; Acts 7: 9). The same is true of flattery, toadyism, and sycophancy (Job 32: 21, 22; Prov. 26: 28; Acts 12: 22; Jas. 2: 3), the motive thereof being always selfish and mean. So also covetousness in an evil sense—a desire to deprive others of their rightful possessions and privileges. Hence, if an individual or class, either by violence or by a process of civil law, by professional beggary, by extortionate prices, by monopolies of labor or capital, by borrowing without means or intention of repayment, by pandering to worldly lust, or by any other dishonest stealth, seeks to persuade or compel others to share their possessions with him, he is in spirit and in fact a thief, seeking to reap where he has not strewn,

and knowing not to do right (Amos 3: 10).
But it is not covetous in a true sense to desire
equal opportunities with others of acquiring
equal possessions with them (1 Cor. 12: 31);
nor is it trespass for anyone to seek to compel
by lawful means others who wilfully withhold
such opportunities to share them with him.

In short all iniquity—that is, inequity or enforced inequality—is robbery (Prov. 11: 1; 22:
22, 23; Ezek. 18: 5-9, 25, 29-31; Matt. 24:
12; Col. 4: 1); also false witness, which includes every example of selfishness; all slander,
avarice, parsimony, thriftlessness, wilful ignorance, brutality, cruelty, or other social inequity
(Ps. 50: 18-20; 62: 10; Gal. 5: 15). "If one
says he loves God, and hateth his brother, he is
a liar" (1 John 4: 20); and every selfish person hates his brother (1 John 3: 17), and every
liar is a cheat and a thief, every falsehood being
a stealthy device to promote some selfish end
(John 8: 44). And as everything false is truth
perverted to evil purposes—all evil being perverted good,—and as the unprecedented advancement of the present age in the increase of
wealth, knowledge, and intelligence is accompanied with a corresponding increase of selfishness that perverts its wealth, knowledge, intelligence to evil purposes—it is the most untruth-

ful, dishonest, and thievish period in the world's history. Its thieves, endowed as they are with wonderful intellectual acumen and scientific skill, surpass any that ever existed before in the multitude and ingenuity of their devices of trickery, fraud and robbery. And the more educated, refined, respectable, zealous in business, politics, or religion they make themselves to appear, the greater are their opportunities of deception and thievery. In fact the greatest thieves have come to be regarded as the most successful men. If one can, as many do, get his living, make himself rich, or secure a fat office in church or state, by fraud, and escape the prison, he is regarded and respected as a man of real genius, and fawned upon by a multitude of flatterers, toadies, and sycophants. Why should he not be when the worship of mammon has become an all-absorbing passion?

Except an honest man flee, as did the prophets of old, into the wilderness to escape persecution (Jer. 9: 1-6), he can hardly avoid falling into the hands of thieves and robbers; and though we fancy that, had we lived in the days of our fathers, we would not have been guilty of their brutalities (Matt. 23: 30), no age has been guilty of so great refinements of cruelty as this. Vast multitudes are enslaved, tortured and murdered by our heartless greed of money —most of which is of sweat and blood wrung from the poor by compelling them to devote their whole strength and life to ceaseless toil, not only to obtain scant food and clothing, but also to support the rich in extravagance, luxury, and ease—crowded into miserable tenements and hovels to die of cold, filth, disease, and starvation, that others may dwell in palaces. And even the great multitudes of the middle classes, regarded as comparatively happy, are plundered and robbed without mercy—almost every breath of air and draught of water being poisoned by the germs of disease evolved and developed of the filthy and unnatural conditions and necessities of our social and business life,—cheated by adulterated foods and drinks, shoddy clothing, and almost every other article of necessity and comfort debased by monopolies in trade and manufacture for purposes of increase and exorbitant profits; also by oppressive taxation through political thievery, and even in free-will offerings for wasted charities and worse than useless rites and ceremonials of worship.

Nevertheless, as it is always darkest just before dawn, we may believe that these great excesses of thievery—resulting, as they have, from our great increase of wealth and knowledge largely perverted to selfish ends—are the immediate precursors of a great reformation. Through the discipline of its great sufferings society is rapidly coming to the consciousness of its own selfishness and inequity and to a willingness to submit to that higher discipline required for the culture and increase of Christian faith, hope, and charity, whereby all social injustice and oppression will be removed—when inequity will no longer be drawn "with cords of vanity, and sin as it were with a cart rope," when evil will no longer be called good, and good evil; nor darkness be put for light, and light for darkness; nor bitter for sweet, and sweet for bitter (Isa. 5: 18–20) ; when the gospel of glad tidings will be preached to the poor, liberty be proclaimed to the captive, and the prison door opened to them that are bound (Isa. 61: 1).

BOOK FOURTH.

APPLIED CHRISTIANITY.

"And Peter, fastening his eyes upon him with John, said, 'Look on us.' And he gave heed unto them, expecting to receive something from them. Then Peter said, 'Silver and gold have I none, but such as I have give I thee. In the name of Jesus Christ of Nazareth, rise up and walk.' And he lifted him up. And immediately his feet and ankle bones received strength, and he, leaping up, stood and walked, and entered with them into the temple, walking and leaping and praising God."—Acts 3: 4-8.

PROLOGUE.

A PARADOX is a tenet, proposition, illustration, or teaching which is true, but appears to the untruthful to be false ; is wise, but appears to the unwise as foolish and absurd ; is in harmony with divine life and order, but to the disobedient appears in conflict therewith ; is practical, but to those who have no faith in, or sympathy with, the truth it teaches, appears impractical, inexpedient, or even fanatical.

Naturally we judge by appearances, and, if we were what we should be, appearances would always represent what is true,—that is, truth would always appear to be truth—and a paradox would be to us a plain statement of truth ; but to the degree our nature and art are perverted our senses are correspondingly perverted, and we call what is true false, and what is false true (Isa. 5: 20). True religion, therefore, is to false religion or irreligion paradoxical ; and if Christianity be the true religion its teachings must necessarily appear to a sinful

231

world, so far as such teachings are not believed
in, as contradictory and absurd. To the unbe-
liever even the Christ himself is a paradox—a
man, yet making himself God (John 10: 33);
the Son of Man, yet also the Son of God (Matt.
8: 20; 27: 43); living only a brief earthly
life, yet in the beginning with God (John 1:
1, 2; 8: 58); tempted in all things like as we
are, yet without sin(Heb. 4: 15); our Master,
yet our servant (Matt. 23: 10; Phil. 2: 7);
the Lord our Righteousness, yet a friend of
publicans and sinners (Jer. 23: 6; Luke 7:
34); the promised Messiah and King of Glory
(Ps. 24: 10; Dan. 9: 25), yet born in a stable,
cradled in a manger, and crucified as a male-
factor (Luke 2: 7; 23: 33); saving others, yet
not able to save himself (Mark 15: 31); leaving his disciples alone, yet with them always
unto the end of the world (Matt. 28: 20);
dead, yet alive forevermore (Rev. 1: 18).

Although his avowed mission was not to destroy but to fulfill the law (Matt. 5: 17), he
yet forbade his disciples to enforce it among
themselves, or even to resist any transgressions
of their rights (Matt. 38: 39). Heralded as the
Prince of Peace (Isa. 9: 6), he yet declared
that he came not to send peace on the earth,
but a sword (Matt. 10: 34, 36).

So also, to all who judge by appearances, and not by righteous judgment, and who walk by sight rather than by faith,—that is, who interpret by the letter, and not by the spirit—most principles and precepts of his gospel seem contradictory, absurd, and impractical,—as that we receive as we give (Matt. 19: 21 ; Luke 6: 38); what we lose we gain, and what we gain we lose (Matt. 16: 25); are wise in our foolishness, and foolish in our wisdom (11: 25; 1 Cor. 1: 19, 20, 21); made blind by what we see (John 9: 39), and deaf by what we hear (Matt. 13: 13); unrighteous by our righteousness (Matt. 23: 28; Luke 18: 13, 14), enslaved by our freedom (John 8: 32–36; 2 Pet. 2: 19); happy through persecution and suffering (Matt. 5: 11; 1 Pet. 3: 14); strong through our weakness (Joel 3: 10; 2 Cor. 12: 9); glorified through our infirmities (John 12: 23; 2 Cor. 11: 30); religious through our irreligion (Matt. 23: 2–10; Acts 17; 22); orthodox through our heresies (Acts 24: 14); rich through our poverty; comforted through our sorrows; ennobled and exalted through our humility and meekness; filled through hungerings and thirstings (Matt. 5: 2–8); masters through servitude (Matt. 20: 27); must be born again—as if we could enter a second time into our mother's

womb and be born (John 3: 3-5); and except
we eat of his flesh and drink of his blood we
have no life—as if he could give us his flesh to
eat (John 6: 52, 53).

When he said to the unbelieving Jews, "Because I tell you the truth ye believe me not,"
he uttered a truth which seemed to them absurd, so blinded were they by their bigotry and
self-righteousness. Truth to their prejudiced
conscience appeared to be false and vicious, and
for this reason, that as prejudice is ignorance
through a selfish indisposition to know and do
what is right, and as all ideas and objects to a
heart and mind thus perverted are correspondingly perverted, truth is rejected because it is
the truth (John 8: 45). In this way our natural conscience, or love of what is right, becomes unnatural and love of what is unrighteous, so that when we think we hear and see
the truth we are deaf and blind thereto ; think
we are orthodox, are heretics ; sincere, are hypocrites ; clean, are full of extortion and excess ;
honest, are thieves ; charitable, are mean and
miserly ; worshippers of God, are idolaters ;
virtuous, are adulterers ; love God and our
neighbor, disobey the one, and oppress the
other ; rich and happy, yet in fact poor and
miserable ; saved, are lost ; liberal, are churls ;

patriotic citizens, enemies of good government; practical, are vainly fighting against God and our own best interests.

Whatever teaches the truth is true, whether it be history, paradox, parable, or miracle— though, if interpreted only in the letter, it may be, and practically is, untrue. Indeed everything is untrue if interpreted in the letter only; for it is the letter that killeth and the spirit only that giveth life (John 6: 63; 2 Cor. 3: 6). Thus if we interpret eating to be only the masticating and swallowing of food, then are Christ's words, "He that eateth me, even he shall live by me," a hard saying, absurd and offensive; but if we mean the medium and source of life—which is the true idea of eating—then are they true, the body of Christ being in fact the medium and source of our spiritual life, and the eating thereof the partaking of that life. So, too, when he said, "Before Abraham was I am," he uttered an untruth, if our idea of existence be limited to the duration of our brief earthly life—for he was not yet fifty years old; but as an assertion of his original and eternal sonship in God the Father, from whom all true and real sonship in the spirit is derived, this declaration was strictly true (John 8: 56–58).

The highest refinements of conscience, reason, and emotion cannot be expressed in the unrefined speech of men who judge by appearances—superficially, by things as they seem to their unrefined nature, and not by things as they really are. Hence to such men spiritual truths—and by spiritual truths we mean original and practical principles, those which are theoretically true, and may and should be put in practice—must be taught chiefly by paradox, parable, and miracle in which they are shadowed forth—things unseen by things seen—howbeit, when we no longer see through a glass darkly, they may be discerned face to face (John 16: 25; 1 Cor. 13: 12). Indeed it is impossible that the Christ should have taught his truths in any other way to persons whose natural sympathies and instincts of conscience were corrupted and perverted by sin and selfishness (Isa. 6: 9, 10; Matt. 4: 11, 12). All merely literal interpreters of scripture are those who having eyes to see see not, and having ears to hear hear not; and even though they think they believe its paradoxes, parables, and miracles, they are really blind and deaf to them, not being able to discern spiritually, or practically apply, the truths they are designed to teach. Hence in interpreting to his disciples the parable of the Sower, the Christ said, "Unto you"—that is, unto those who were in sympathy with his spirit, and were willing to put his precepts in practice—"it is given to know the mysteries of the Kingdom of God" —that is, the social polity, unity, boundless life, and unselfish love thereof—"but to others in parables." Not, however, that he did not wish others to understand, for he sought to save all men, but that,—in the same sense in which God is said to have hardened Pharaoh's heart by giving the opportunity of repentance, which Pharaoh rejected,—they were so selfish they rejected the truths taught in his parables because they were truths.

It is of course necessary to our salvation that spiritual truths should be illustrated and taught, yet if rejected through our selfish aversion thereto, and regarded as impractical, our hearts are thereby hardened, and we are made spiritually blind and deaf.

Doubtless there are many who profess to believe, and in a literal and historic sense do believe, in this plain and practical parable of the Sower,—for it is not at all incredible that a sower should have gone forth to sow,—but they are so devoted to the world, the flesh, and the devil, and so blinded thereby, that they cannot discern its practical teachings or apply them to their own salvation. Not realizing that it is the devil of selfishness in their own hearts that catches away and devours the good seed; that there is such lack of the moisture of human sympathy and of the Christian spirit of self-sacrifice for the salvation of others that the love of God and their neighbor can find no root therein; and however otherwise good and kind, the cares of this world and the deceitfulness of riches so choke the word that it can bring no fruit to perfection. While in theory they may believe in the Christian religion, and become even zealous church members, their zeal is not according to knowledge; and through selfishness or the stress of physical necessities such as every poor clergyman is subjected to, they are either unwilling or unable to apply practically the faith they profess to the just and equitable adjustment of social interests and relations.

The same is true of the parable of the Prodigal Son—the rich and extravagant not realizing that they are spending their substance in riotous living, nor the profligate poor that they are tending swine and feeding on husks. So also the parables of the Talents and of the Unjust Steward are riddles to the miserly rich and the thriftless poor—the one laying up his treasures in a napkin, wherein there can be no increase that can benefit himself or others; and the other, however otherwise honest he may be, less wise, prudent, and enterprising than those who by dishonest means seek to promote their selfish interests, not realizing that the unrighteous mammon may be converted to righteousness, become the friend of the poor, and made to promote our spiritual interests.

In like manner, what is true of a merely literal interpretation of parables is true also of a like interpretation of miracles,—many regarding them as signs and wonders (John 4: 48), as magic rather than miracle, and designed to inspire superstitious awe rather than to teach practical truths. There are no magic arts, no sorceries, no juggleries in God's works, though all are miracles so far as they surpass our finite comprehensions and powers. Nor is God or his works ever supernatural—there being no such word in his books of inspiration— but always natural, howbeit the natural and spiritual differ from each other only as divine nature and art. None of the mighty works wrought by the Christ, his prophets, or apostles were unnatural, or contrary to eternal and fixed principles of law and order; nor where

any of them wrought to show us what he can
do, but what we can do by his help; and to the
degree of our faith in and obedience to such
eternal and fixed principles are all things possible to us (Mark 3: 15; 9: 23; Luke 10: 19).
Like paradoxes and parables all miracles are
true that teach the truth; and though, because
of our ignorance or perversion of God's truth,
and because we walk by sight rather than by
faith, they seem contrary to nature, they are in
fact wholly in accordance therewith.   Thus,
while we are fighting the battles of life, and
striving for victory over our enemies, the sun
really stands still (Josh. 10: 12, 13)—nay, by
its apparent motions, whereby our lives are
measured for days and years, it is really waiting for us to accomplish the missions God has
sent us into the world to accomplish; even its
shadow made to go back on the dial (2 Kings
20: 8-11), when we repent us of our sin and
selfishness, and would reform our lives.   So
also in fact are we born again in spirit, when
we put away selfishness and are willing to deny
ourselves, take up our cross, and really follow
the Christ in spirit and in truth (Matt. 10: 38,
39; John 3: 7, 8); the water is turned to the
new wine of life (John 2: 9); the chains
stricken from our limbs, and the iron gate made

to open of itself (Acts 12: 6, 10); cloven tongues of fire to descend upon us (Acts 2: 3); and in short all things to become possible and practicable—every disease and infirmity healed, every social wrong righted, and every social problem solved, if we really believe and put in practice the gospel of the Christ. Thus, if we have the faith of Peter and John, there is no doubt at all that we can take every poor cripple by the hand whom we can inspire with a like faith, lift him up, set him on his feet, and lead him in at the Beautiful Gate, walking, leaping, and praising God.

But no miracles can be wrought through the spirit of repentance for the remission of sins, no valley filled, no mountain or hill brought low, and no crooked path or rough way be made straight or smooth, except we be inspired with such a spirit, and capable of comprehending and practically realizing its purpose. As defined by the great Forerunner of our Lord, this spirit is filial and brotherly kindness, and its purpose social reform (Luke 3: 11–14). No person can be counted a repentant sinner, or come near to the Kingdom of God, if having two coats he is unwilling to impart to him that hath none, or having meat is unwilling to do likewise, exacts more than is justly his due, injures others by violence or falsehood, or is not content with what he earns. Nor can he without hypocrisy utter the Lord's Prayer— say in sincerity, " Our Father," or " Forgive us our debts," except he show his faith by his works for the practical recognition of the universal Fatherhood of God and the Brotherhood of Man.

PART I.

"Now faith is the substance of things hoped for, the evidence of things not seen " (Heb. 11 : 1, 3). That is, as in God the Substance is the ultimate and unseen element of his Being, from which all substantives—that is, things seen,—are derived, and whereby all principles comprehended in divine Nature and Art are made manifest in outward and visible things, so is Christian faith the substance, that is, the ultimate element or principle of the invisible Kingdom of God, whereby the substantive, outward, and visible Kingdom or Church of Christ in the world is made to appear, all its hopes and promises inspired, and all its charities practically applied and realized in our social life. It is, therefore, both theoretical and practical —the assurance subjectively of the reality of things hoped for, and the proving objectively that such unseen realities may be outwardly experienced. And if, as we believe, this faith is the fundamental element of true religion, of the bond of unity between God and Man, it is

the ideal conception of what our social relations
should be, and the assurance that we may live
together in this world in obedience to God,
and in peace and good will toward each other.
Practically applied, it is our effort to articulate
this ideal conception in our outward and visible
social life by the reformation and improvement
of society; and the first step therein is the
establishment of a social institution called the
Church—a society, congregation, or school,
organized to illustrate, teach, and practice the
principles of the gospel of the Christ. As
originally constituted, it represented a social
compact in which each member was pledged to
love God with all his heart, mind, and soul, and
his neighbor as himself—which pledge was a
practical recognition of the Fatherhood of God
and the Brotherhood of Man. With this idea,
and this only, is it possible rightly to apply the
Christian Faith. In such compact, and such
only, can our ultimate salvation be realized;
for manifestly the unseen Kingdom and Household of God which the true Church represents
—that is, is its evidence and proving—must be
a community in which the well-being of its
members is perfected through their love of God
and each other (Matt. 5: 45; Luke 10: 25–28;
Gal. 5: 14, 15; Jas. 2: 8, 9).

As now applied, however, the original and true idea of faith is much obscured in the congregation of the Church, it being largely perverted and limited to a belief in merely speculative and sectarian dogmas or articles of faith, so called, more fanciful than real or practical, and whether speculatively true or false, not essential to our social well-being—so that if the whole nation, or all nations, were included in such congregations, the Church would be very far from representing a community of Christian brethren—would "have the faith of our Lord Jesus Christ in respect of persons" (Jas. 2: 1). Any faith, however true, is merely speculative, which is not practically applied, or is misapplied; and any church is sectarian, however true in the letter, that is not true also in spirit to the principles of the gospel. While the spirit and purpose of the Christ were to bring all men into his one Kingdom, so that there should be but one Fold and one Shepherd, his Church on earth, which claims to represent that Kingdom, is divided into many and mutually exclusive folds, presided over by many shepherds, and representing many and diverse faiths—practically anti-christian in spirit and purpose (Mark 13: 21, 22).

The first requisite, therefore, to the practical

application of the faith we profess is that it should itself be conformed with the original faith. Being corrupted, it must be transformed by the renewing of its mind, that it may prove what is the good, acceptable, and perfect will of God (Rom. 12: 2); for otherwise—except it realize in' its own congregations its social ideal —it is conformed to the world, and it is impossible that it should be applied to the world's redemption.

To this end the congregations of the Church must be reformed and transformed into one Body in Christ, and become severally members one of another (5). Its faith must become such as leads each member to cherish as his own the well-being of his fellow-members, for otherwise it cannot be or represent the Family of God. All members must strive to attain the best gifts, privileges, and personal endowments (1 Cor. 12: 31), and share the benefits thereof equally—that is justly—with each other as each has need (Deut. 15: 7–11; 1 Cor. 12: 4–31; 1 John 3: 17). Otherwise we are Christians only in name (Prov. 30: 8, 9; Jas. 2: 7, 8, 9), our spirit selfish and worldly, our worship idolatrous and adulterous (Ezek. 23: 37; Col. 3: 5), and our promises vain and delusive (Matt. 19: 24; Jas. 1: 27).

Now as Peter and John were members of the original Church, and had been immediate disciples and followers of the Christ, they no doubt clearly understood his philosophy, and in spirit and purpose were in full sympathy with him. Having listened to his teachings and witnessed his works—all of which were for the improvement of our social condition, healing the sick and preaching the Kingdom of God (Luke 9 : 2)—they not only believed them to be true, but embraced every opportunity to illustrate and apply them to the solution of social problems. Why should not we, who profess the same faith, work the same works? If the gospel was true and practical in their day, it certainly must be now in our age of unprecedented enlightenment, in which the most powerful nations of the earth have, theoretically at least, accepted its principles as the true religious faith. Although the evil spirits of bigotry, intolerance, and superstition still linger in the churches, and they are otherwise greatly corrupted by cupidity and worldliness, yet no person can doubt, who discerns and rightly interprets the signs of the times, that the fullness of time has come for the practical reformation of the faith we profess in its restoration to its original singleness of purpose, and its applica-

tion to the right solution of all social problems.
As "unto the pure, all things are pure, but
unto them who are defiled and unbelieving
is nothing pure," so to the practical all things
are practical that are just and equitable; and
if any persons claiming to be Christians do not
believe the practical application of the gospel
to be practicable, " they profess that they know
God, but in works they deny him, being abom-
inable, disobedient, and to every good work
reprobate " (Titus 1: 15, 16). Of course a
selfishly rich man, or an envious poor man, or
any other willful moth, rust, or thief, except he
repent and bring forth works meet for repentance, will not regard the practical application
of the gospel as practicable—interpreting
"practical" to mean only such enterprises as
promote his selfish and worldly interests and
desires. But no man who believes he can repent, and does repent, will doubt that others
may also. In fact, this is the real test of the
genuineness of our faith—whether we so believe that we are willing to put it in practice;
for if one professes to believe and is yet unwilling to practice, he is practically a hypocrite.

But what is practical is not always expedient
—never is expedient in fact except to the degree we believe it to be practicable. That is, it

is not expedient to attempt to put in practice
any truth except to the degree it has been
heralded, taught, and accepted as truth—although the true prophet will himself strive to
practice what he preaches. Thus the Christ
did not appear until the fullness of time had
come—till his coming had been heralded, his
way prepared (Matt. 11: 10; Luke 3: 4, 5;
Gal. 4: 4, 5). A child must be fed with milk,
and not with meat, till it is able to bear it (1
Cor. 3: 2). Only so far as the spirit of truth
rules our hearts can we know or hear the truth,
(John 16: 12, 13). "All things," says St.
Paul, "are lawful unto me, but all things are
not expedient" (1 Cor. 6: 12). Hence, while
community in unity is always practicable to
truly Christian men, it is never expedient or
possible to practice it in a congregation of selfish and world-minded people (1 Cor. 6: 15)—
such congregation not being really Christian.
But if the congregation be sincerely striving to
know and represent the true Church, however
otherwise imperfect, it is always both practicable and expedient.

Now it being manifestly impossible that there
should be community without unity—mutual
love and helpfulness while there are divisions
among us (1 Cor. 10: 13),—the original church

to which Peter and John belonged must have
represented community in unity—"one Lord,
one faith, one baptism, One God and Father of
all, who is above all, and through all, and in
you all " (Eph. 4: 2-6). Otherwise it could not
have represented the Christ who was himself
the Church (Eph. 3: 10; 5: 30; Col. 1: 24)—
the true "Vine," of which his Father was the
husbandman, and all true disciples the branches
(John 15: 1-5)—the community in unity of
God with Man, and of men with men.

Moreover, as the Kingdom of God cometh
not by observation,—that is, not primarily by
erecting a building and gathering a congregation, and saying, lo! here is the Church, but by
the development of faith within us,—it is plain
that community in unity does not consist in
statutes and ordinances of man's appointment
(Eph. 2: 15, 16; Col. 2: 14, 20; Heb. 9: 10),
but in voluntary and inward conformity in
spirit with the teachings and example of the
Christ, whereby like our Master we fulfill the
will of God outwardly in the world (Matt. 10:
25; Heb. 10: 7). In fact the gospel, so far as
it is believed in and put in practice, is itself the
abolition of all statutes and ordinances, and
confers upon every true member of God's
Household unlimited freedom of thought and

action. It is wholly of love, and not at all of law, though love is the fulfilling of the law, and in perfect love is perfect obedience. So far then, and only so far, as we can live together without law, loving God and each other, are we possessed of a true faith in Christ, and members of his Church, or is there any unity and community in faith. Nay, so long as they teach for doctrines the commandments of men (Isa. 29: 13; Ezek. 33: 31, 32; Matt. 15: 8, 9), it is but hypocrisy, a mere pretence of being brethren, for differing sects to hold union meetings, sit at each other's tables, break the same bread and drink the same cup,—merely drawing near to God and each other with their mouths, and honoring him with their lips, while their hearts are far from him. Hence, if we would have a true and practical unity, and would rightly apply it to the reformation of the Church, all compulsory creeds and articles of faith of man's appointment, whereby professing Christians are divided into narrow and opposing sects, must be abolished. In fact, so long as any congregation is under ecclesiastical statutes and ordinances, it is not a church of Christ, but is still under the law, and at best only a Jewish synagogue.

The only essential requisite to baptism is a

sincere desire to be baptized in public recognition of the Fatherhood of God and the Brotherhood of Man, and in testimony of practical
unity and community of life in the spirit.   And
the only heresy or cause of excommunication
is failure to keep God's holy will and commandments in obedience to his laws, and by fulfilling the same in love.   Nor should excommunication be by any process of ecclesiastical law,
there being in fact no such law in the true
Church (Rom. 7: 4–6; Gal. 3: 11–14), whereby
the offender may be tried and condemned.   On
the contrary we are expressly forbidden to
judge each other (Matt. 7: 1; Luke 6: 37;
John 8: 11), and instructed that every transgressor under the gospel should be left to condemn himself (John 3: 17; Titus 3: 10, 11).
To judge others is to condemn ourselves (Rom.
2: 1)—is evidence that while we profess to be
free from the bondage of the law we are still
subject thereto.   Yet every persistently unfaithful member may and should be excommunicated in the way appointed by the Christ, in
which way only what we bind or loose on earth
will be bound or loosed in heaven (Matt. 18:
15–18).

As the design of the gospel is to do away
with the necessity of laws and penalties, the

church cannot consistently make laws and inflict penalties. To attempt to enforce its principles is to abandon its principles, and to render our profession of love vain and hypocritical. Indeed the special mission of the Christ, as St. Paul declares, is to abolish the law of commandments in ordinances (Eph. 2: 15), blotting out the handwriting thereof, and nailing it to the cross (Col. 2: 14). "Wherefore if ye be dead with Christ from the rudiments of the world, why, as though living in the world, are ye subject to ordinances (touch not, taste not, handle not, which all are to perish in the using) after the doctrines and commandments of men" (Col. 20: 21, 22)? Manifestly, so long as the church is subject to such ordinances, it is enslaved, narrow, illiberal, all freedom of thought, enterprise, and aspiration limited and repressed, and its true spirit and purpose—which is to deliver its members from the "bondage of corruption into the glorious liberty of the children of God"—perverted into a system of tyranny and oppression (Isa. 32: 5, 8 ; 2 Cor. 3: 17; Gal. 5: 1-6).

This, therefore, is the one and only possible solution of the problem of church or Christian unity, whereby all diverse and hostile sects may be united in one body in Christ—not by any compromise or agreement in any system of dogmatic theology of man's appointment, forms of worship, or canon laws, but by abolishing all such ecclesiasticisms, and returning to the original, free, and voluntary system and polity of the Kingdom of God ordained by the Christ, "that they all may be one as Thou, Father, art in me, and I in Thee, that they also may be one in us; that the world may believe that Thou hast sent me." Oneness is unity in liberty, and there can be no greater error than to suppose it can be secured under the enforced compulsion and restrictions of canon laws (John 8: 36; Gal. 4: 26; 5: 1).

Peter and John were united in faith—one with their Master in spirit and purpose—but knew nothing of creeds or canon laws in the modern sense, each teaching the philosophy of the gospel as he understood it, and in his own way—differing no doubt in unessential matters, and in the circumstances and necessities of their special missions, yet in perfect harmony in all essential things, each preaching the same gospel, and illustrating the same faith by his works. Each recognized the other as his brother in the church, and labored with him to the same end—the fulfilling of the law in love in the unity and community of Man with God,

and of men with men. Their idea of organic
unity was in the community of faith and works,
and not at all in the commandments and ordinances of men. In fact there was no church
in their day in the sense it is supposed to exist
now,—no Kingdom of God that had come from
observation; although, being developed of faith,
its presence in the world was practically revealed in visible signs, and realized in congregations or brotherhoods.

Now when our faith is thus practically applied to the restoration of unity, the church
will be in a position to subject the world unto
itself,—to illustrate and teach by its own example what true liberty, equality, and fraternity are, to heal all infirmities, right all wrongs,
and remove all social oppressions. It will be
one body in Christ (1 Cor. 10: 17), wasting nothing in internal dissensions,—no time, strength,
or money in partisan zeal, in dogmatic wran-
glings, in heathenish, sensational, or spectacular
rites or ceremonials, or other extravagances and
dissipations, but recognizing what things are
true in all religions, and utilizing them for the
promotion of the one and only true religion;
proving all things, and holding fast that which
is good; forgetting what is behind, and press-

ing toward the mark for the prize of the high
calling of God in Christ Jesus.

When such unity in community is established,
all things, so far as regards the church itself,
will become practical and expedient; for there
is no doubt at all that both clergy and laity can
voluntarily distribute their incomes, whether
of money, knowledge, experience, privileges,
comforts, or necessities among themselves as
they have need—not grudgingly or of necessity, but cheerfully, knowing that they shall
receive as they give in full measure, pressed
down and running over (Luke 6: 38; 2 Cor.
9: 6, 7; Gal. 6: 10).   Otherwise—if we do
not give as we receive—our light will not shine
before men, and we cannot win them to the true
Church (Matt. 5: 16)—cannot lay up treasures
in heaven or ourselves enter therein (Matt. 6:
19, 20; 7: 21).   In fact, without such unity
in community we are self-condemned and excommunicated, though we still remain nominally members of the church, not being Christian in spirit or in truth.   Nor can any domes-
tic, social, business, or political interests or
considerations excuse us from this first and
paramount duty which all members of the
church owe to each other—that of mutual love
and helpfulness, which is the bond of true re-

ligion in the Church of Christ (Matt. 6: 33; 10: 37, 38; Luke 14: 18, 19).

But if it be said that rich men will not enter the church, if they are required to share their incomes equally with their poorer brethren, we answer unhesitatingly, that if such men keep aloof through such a selfish motive, they are neither wanted in the church, nor can be justly permitted to enter; for "it is easier for a camel to go through the eye of a needle," than for them to enter the Kingdom of God. Of such it is said, "Woe unto you that are rich, for ye have received your consolation. Woe unto you that are full, for ye shall hunger. Woe unto you that laugh now, for ye shall mourn and weep." But the rich are as capable of becoming unselfish—that is, "poor in spirit" (Matt. 5: 3; Jas. 1: 9, 10)—as are the poor; and no doubt many will gladly embrace their opportunity to lay up their treasures in heaven. Nor is it true as many suppose, that all business enterprise would be suppressed among members of the church, were community in unity established, but on the contrary it would be increased; for unselfishness—that is, love—in a Christian breast is a higher and stronger motive than selfishness, as is strikingly illustrated in the parable of the Talents (Matt. 25: 15–31);

and when we realize that our riches are put out
at usury by distributing them among our brethren in Christ as they have need, and are thereby
not only saved but increased and utilized to
our eternal well-being, our desire to acquire
wealth will be encouraged and stimulated that
we may have the more to give (Acts 20: 35;
Eph. 4: 28).

In like manner it may be said that many
thriftless persons will seek entrance in order to
secure a livelihood without personal exertion;
but if any enter through such motive they may
be easily detected and excommunicated by
withholding from them all contributions—thus
treating them as our Master has directed (Matt.
18: 15–18).

Doubtless, also, many clergymen, from selfish motives, will oppose community, lest, if
denominationalism be done away, they be
thereby deprived of their livings, a less number
than is now required being deemed sufficient.
And certainly a less number will be required
in localities where the church has been already
established, though many more than are now
employed will be required in other localities.
Thus a small town that now supports the
church organizations of many denominations
will need but one; and the money thus saved

will enable it to send as many or more missionaries—and all true clergymen are missionaries
—into other fields as it now supports at home.
If there be a will to bring about any reformation, there is always a way, and if there be any
Christianity left in the churches, it is certain
that its faith can be practically applied to the
restoration of community in unity; howbeit
much patience must be exercised before this
can be realized, so many are the sects, and so
great are the prejudices, superstitions, and
bigotries—moths, rust, and thieves—that have
been developed therein. But if any denomi-
nation, or single congregation, can be so reformed as to represent the original spirit and
purpose of the church, it will ultimately gather
to itself all other denominations and congregations. Let the ministry lead the way in this
movement, as it certainly can if it will—nay
certainly will, if it be not simply a horde of
parasites—sharing equally with each other its
incomes, and the laity will ultimately follow its
example. Whereupon, being assured of a livelihood for itself and its families, there will be no
occasion for lack of moral courage, and it can
boldly and efficiently preach the gospel of glad
tidings to the poor, and the opening of every
prison door of social injustice and oppression.

Otherwise it is impossible for it to become ensamples to or feed the flock of Christ (1 Pet. 5 : 2, 3).

Indeed it is impossible to conceive of a more abject and pitiable condition of thralldom, meanness, and beggary than that of a clergyman who, through the stress of temporal necessities, feels compelled to limit his faith to a narrow and bigoted dogmatic and sectarian theology, to win proselytes to his sect, and waste his time and exhaust his zeal in going from house to house pulling door bells, in social gossip, in formal pietisms, in obsequious and servile flatteries and toadyisms. Doubtless it would be more honorable to earn one's living by tent-making or any other useful employment than by ministering to the fancies and tastes of a world-minded congregation. But really it is more the fault of the clergy than the laity that they have become so enthralled that they dare not, if they would, preach the true and practical gospel of liberty, equality, and fraternity, being in a condition of base servility through their own selfishness and narrow mindedness, whereby faith in creeds of their own appointment has been substituted for faith in the gospel of liberty—thereby creating schisms, fomenting strife, and suppressing their own natural spirit of manliness and independence. And as usual in such cases, the innocent suffer for the guilty,—the true apostles and prophets, being cast out as heretics and driven into the wilderness, while the mere time-servers who preach to please the fancies of the people remain to enjoy the loaves and fishes—the thirty pieces of silver they receive for the betrayal of their Master—not realizing that he who seeks to save his life loses it, and he who loses it for the sake of the gospel saves it (Matt. 10: 39; 16: 25). So far, and only so far, as we sustain each other, sharing with each other equitably all our incomes, can we with boldness preach the Kingdom of God, or ourselves become inheritors thereof. We must put our money in one bag, as did the immediate disciples of the Christ. Otherwise we are tempted, and most of us really compelled like the Pharisees, to compass sea and land to make proselytes (Matt. 23: 15), that we may keep up our slender salaries, while others receive much more than they need, thus making themselves objects of envy among their poorer brethren.

Now while every individual member of the Church is permitted to hold the titles to his own property and give as he pleases, yet if he does not give all he can afford, or is necessary

and expedient, he cannot be a member. Hence
it is necessary that each member should clearly
understand what he can afford and what is expedient to be given.   This, however, cannot be
determined by any fixed rule of proportion, but
in the unselfish conscience of the Church by
the varying necessities of its members—although
no member should permit himself to enjoy any
greater opportunities and privileges of improvement, or of comforts and enjoyments, than
another.   Nor in order to secure such equality
will it be necessary always for all to give their
entire incomes to the church; for if all are
temperate and industrious, refraining from all
extravagances, useless luxuries, or dissipations,
many can accumulate wealth whereby their incomes are increased, and they will have the
more to give as the necessities arising from the
increased culture and refinement of the congregation are developed.

Like all other works of God the true Church
is a development of divine Art in harmony with
natural, moral, and spiritual laws.   Hence its
organization—and necessarily it must have organization, as have all works of God, else there
would be no authority, order, economy, coher-
ence, or continuity therein—must be such as
will best promote the purpose for which it is

designed. Representing the body of Christ
(Matt. 26 : 26 ; Rom. 12 : 5), it must be "fitly
joined together and compacted by that which
every joint supplieth according to the effectual
working in the measure of every part, making
increase of the body unto the edifying of itself
in love " (Eph. 4 : 16), and "growing up into a
holy temple in the Lord." It must also have a
mind receptive of knowledge (Hos. 4 : 6 ; 1
Cor. 1 : 5 ; Col. 2 : 3), a heart beating in sympathy with all human suffering (Luke 4 : 18 ;
1 Pet. 3 : 8), and the spirit of obedience to
God's will (Heb. 10 : 7 ; 1 John 2 : 17). And
as we have many members in one body, and all
have not the same office, there must necessarily
be orders in the church, representing the differing gifts of its members and their varying duties and works (Eph. 4 : 11, 12), each coveting
the best gifts, and exercising authority to the
degree of his natural and cultured abilities—
howbeit no authority may be exercised arbitrarily or capriciously. And as each member
voluntarily subjects himself to the higher powers (Rom. 13 : 1–11), there will be harmony and
coöperation, and all things will be done decently
and in order (1 Cor. 14 : 40).

But it is supposed—and herein lies a radical
error of the churches of our day—that the

necessary organization thereof, and the establishment of the orders essential to their efficiency, unity, and continuity, must be brought about and enforced by canon laws; yet as there were no such laws in the original church, and as that church is manifestly the true model by which all should be constructed, it is plain that such laws are not only unnecessary, but are inconsistent with the spirit of the gospel. Indeed, to the degree they are found to be essential—that is, so far as a voluntary compact cannot otherwise be maintained—is the congregation corrupted, and has ceased to be a church.

Naturally the men who first followed the Christ at his bidding were called apostles, and became the chief missionaries. As chief missionaries they also naturally became overseers, that is, bishops of the congregations they established, as did also the missionaries that succeeded them. What is now called a diocese or synod originally comprised the congregations which the missionary established and the localities in which he labored, which naturally recognized him as their overseer. So also the elders were men of age and experience in the congregations, and naturally chosen and ordained as overseers and pastors of the flock (Acts 14: 23; 1 Tim. 5: 17; 1 Pet. 5: 1–6); and the like is true of deacons, prophets, evangelists, pastors and teachers (Eph 4: 11), all of whom were developed as necessity required from the foundation of the apostles, Christ being the chief corner stone (Eph. 2: 20). None, however, were chosen by partiality or for the sake of preferring one above another (1 Tim. 5: 21, 22); nor did any accept office by constraint or for filthy lucre, but of a ready mind; neither as being lords over God's heritage, but being ensamples to the flock (1 Pet. 5: 2, 3).

As all things were common in the original church—that is, held by the individual owners for the common good—there were no salaried offices, all sharing equally with each other, to whatever order he belonged. All being laborers together with God (1 Cor. 3: 9), no distinction seems to have been recognized in official merit between any who did their duty to the best of their abilities, nor did any special privileges, emoluments, perquisites, or honorary titles pertain to any office—each receiving only his penny a day, that is, only what he needed to supply his necessities. In this simple way all social problems pertaining to the equal and just distribution of wealth were solved. Nor is it possible to solve them in any other way, and at the same time entitle us to enter the King-

dom of God, in which all things are common,—
howbeit that in a sinful and selfish world, not
yet subdued to the church, it is manifestly inexpedient and unjust to establish and enforce
community in unity, except to the degree it be
leavened by the spirit of the gospel.

As worship is the culture of religion, it
should be wholly devoted to such culture ; and
as very much of what is called worship is
merely spectacular and ritualistic—merely eye
and lip service, and not in the least conducive
to our social well-being—faith should be applied to its reformation. Thus prayer, which
is an essential element of worship, should be
utilized to the culture of high and pure inspirations and aspirations, teaching what we should
strive to realize in ourselves and others—asking
and seeking of God all good gifts (Matt. 7 :
7, 8), knocking that the door may be opened to
the possession and enjoyment of all riches we
have been unable to realize through our ignorance, sin, and selfishness. While God knoweth
what we need before our asking (Matt. 6 : 8),
yet, aside from the natural gifts he bestows
upon all men (Matt. 5 : 45), nothing more can
be bestowed except we become through personal culture and effort capable of receiving
and enjoying higher gifts. And as nothing is

impossible to him that believeth (Matt. 17:
20), every petition which presents a true ideal
of increased life and enjoyment, if persistently
uttered both in words and deeds, will in due
time be granted. But if we construe persistence in prayer—and we are told to pray without ceasing (1 Thess. 5: 17)—to mean impor-
tunity and excess in lip service, or if we pray
to be seen of men (Matt. 6: 5, 6), or use vain
repetitions (Matt. 6: 7), or ask God to do for
us what we can and should do for ourselves
(Ex. 14: 15; Phil. 2: 12), our prayers are
vain and hypocritical. In short, all true
Christian prayers are outlined in what is
known as the Lord's Prayer, in which we are
taught to recognize the Fatherhood of God, and
our own sonship in him; to reverence and love
him; to promote his Kingdom on earth
through our own unity and brotherhood; to
seek opportunity of earning our daily bread;
to overcome temptation by following his guidance; to forgive as we would be forgiven; and
finally to seek and obtain thereby deliverance
from all evil—all of which manifestly require
for their realization personal effort on our part.

But it is not sufficient to apply our faith to
the reformation of the church. In fact, if it be
so limited, it would be dead, it being perverted

to the exclusive and selfish purpose of securing
the salvation only of its own household—not
differing from that of an individual ruled by a
like motive.   To fulfill the law in love our motive must be that of our Master, who came, not
to condemn the world, but that through him
the world might be saved (John 3 : 17).   This
being the real purpose of the Christ—that
through him the world might be saved—it
must also be that of the Church which is the
body of Christ, and represents his real presence
in the world.   Like the Christ the Christian in
the world is a citizen of the world, howbeit
that in the church his citizenship is in heaven
(Eph. 2 : 19; Phil. 3: 20).   And the same is
true of the Church itself, which, though not of
the world, is yet in the world, subject to the
necessities of the flesh, and needs and receives
protection under the law.   While therefore it
has in itself no necessity of statutes and ordinances of man's appointment, it is necessarily
subject to those of the world, not only for its
own protection from the world, but also to enable it to exert its influence and fulfill its mission therein.   Otherwise it would be entirely
separated from the world which it seeks to redeem and subdue unto itself.   It must be in-
corporated under the civil laws that it may, as

every individual member does, hold its possessions, and carry on its missionary, educational,
and charitable work. All true members will
enter actively into the affairs of secular life
(Rom. 12: 11), not only that they may earn
their own living, but also that they may create
and accumulate riches; and especially into
politics, that they may bring the civil into conformity with the natural and moral laws of
God, whereby all men may be protected in their
natural and lawfully acquired rights and possessions. Not that we should be friends of the
world—in sympathy with its selfishness, vanity,
and worldly pride—for the friendship of the
world is enmity with God (Jas. 4 : 4), but that
we should bring the world into friendship with
the Church. Not that we should love the
world, or the things of the world, to the exclusion of the love of God (1 John 2 : 15), but
that we should *so* love the world that we willingly and gladly undergo any needful sacrifice
to redeem and save it. Not that we should be
fashioned according to the world (1 Cor. 7 : 31),
for the fashion of this world passeth away, and
our effort should be to transform it into the
likeness of the Kingdom of God. And though
we cannot serve God and mammon, we may
transform the mammon of unrighteousness into

a servant of God. In short, as the law is a schoolmaster to bring us to Christ, so must we use it to bring all men to the Church—must subject them to the discipline of the law, and at the same time teach them how they may be redeemed from its bondage—thus rendering "unto Cæsar the things that are Cæsar's, and unto God the things that are God's."

To apply our faith to the redemption of the world is primarily to impart it to the world—which, however, we can never do, though we talk with the tongues of men and of angels (1 Cor. 13: 1), except we manifest a practical sympathy with oppressed and suffering human beings—stop to listen to their cries, fasten our eyes upon them, study their condition, and make practical effort to redeem and save them. If the world is selfish, we must show ourselves unselfish,—unclean, we must be pure—unjust and unmerciful, we must be just and merciful. This was the method of Peter and John when this beggar asked of them an alms. They listened to his cry, stopped and fastened their eyes upon him. Not being mere literalists in the interpretation of the gospel—not simply seeing with their natural eyes, or hearing with their natural ears, but seeing and hearing also in the spirit and purpose of their Master—they recognized in this beggar's cry the voice of God directly appealing unto them, and saying, "I am hungry, I am athirst, I am a stranger, I am naked, I am sick, I am in prison" (Matt. 25: 34–40)—"enter not in at the Beautiful Gate of my Temple without first making every effort and sacrifice to bring in others with you, who by their uncleanness, misfortunes, or infirmities are excluded therefrom." It is also the voice of his church; and any professed believer who is yet blind and deaf to the oppressions and sufferings of his fellow-men—unwilling to give as he has received,—willing to save himself, but unwilling to save others—is dead in faith (Jas. 2: 17–20), and instead of saving his life will lose it, and all other possessions he has thought to save through selfishness will be taken from him (Luke 8: 18).

As no unclean person can enter the Kingdom of God (Eph. 5: 5), any person who supposes himself to be in the church because his name is enrolled in the list of communicants, but who in spirit is indifferent to the injustice and selfishness of society, deceiveth himself, and his religion is vain and hypocritical (Jas. 1: 26, 27),—not being clothed in the wedding garment of loyalty to his Master (Matt. 22: 11). In other words, except we be undefiled with selfish

motives when we are baptized, we are not baptized into the church, our baptism being unchristian.

Now the motive of Peter and John, when
they stopped and fastened their eyes upon this
beggar, was an unselfish desire to help him;
and to this end they sought first to impart their
faith. Had they not stopped, thereby chal-
lenging his attention, and testifying their interest in him, this would have been impossible;
for unless we manifest a personal interest in the
moth, rust, and thief, we cannot exert any religious and personal influence upon them, or
develop any responsive effort on their part to
help themselves; and if we do not fasten our
eyes upon them we cannot study their condition, or devise any practical method for their
redemption. Had they failed to impart their
faith, as well they might—for all social parasites are largely such from the depressing and
brutalizing conditions and influences of a selfish
society of which they have been evolved and
developed, and by which they have become
hopeless of improvement, or utterly indifferent
thereto—they would have passed him by, and
left him to be dealt with and disciplined by the
law (Matt. 10: 14; 18: 34). Having nothing
to impart but their faith, they would have been

powerless to help him through the ministrations of the gospel—from faith being evolved and developed all true hopes and efforts for improvement (Matt 13: 58; Eph. 2: 8).

As comparatively few parasites can be reclaimed by moral suasion only, the chief effort of Christian people should be practically to apply their faith to the improvement and enforcement of the civil laws, whereby such laws may be conformed in spirit and purpose with the natural and moral laws of God ; for otherwise— through our citizenship in the world we being responsible with others for its corrupt and oppressive political conditions—it would be hypocritical for us to exhort sinful men to look unto us and be saved from the social evils which have resulted from such conditions. In fact, it is impossible for any man to be a Christian except he be also a good citizen, doing all he can to promote equitable civil government ; for the fundamental principles of the gospel are the same as those of the natural and moral laws, howbeit that it represents a higher culture thereof. The Church is the true ideal of the nation, a Kingdom ruled in righteousness, and its design is to convert the nation into such a Kingdom. The idea, therefore, that because our citizenship is in heaven we have no responsi-

bility for the political conditions of the nation—
are prohibited, in fact, from meddling with politics—is a radical error, utterly subversive of the
principles of true religion, and opposed to the
express command of our Master, that we should
render unto Cæsar the things that are Cæsar's.
Cæsar is the civil government, without which
in a sinful world there could be no protection
of the church, or of the rights and liberties of
men. He is in the world a higher power (Rom.
13: 1–8; Titus 3: 1), a minister of God for
good, and, however tyrannical, essential to the
world's discipline. To the degree that the
world becomes leavened with the spirit of the
gospel will the civil government be conformed
to the moral law and converted into a school of
Christ.

How then should our faith be applied to the
reformation of the government? Simply and
precisely in the same way that every true
Christian man has applied it to the reformation
of his individual life. As he has been brought
to Christ primarily by obedience to natural and
moral laws, so should he strive to discipline
the government. Cæsar must be taught these
laws and obedience thereto—that his authority
is derived wholly from God, that so far only as
he enacts and enforces these laws for the well-

being of the people governed, and the protection of their rights and liberties, is he a minister of God; and that so far as he neglects to enact and enforce them, or enacts and enforces other laws for the promotion of selfish interests, is he a usurper and a tyrant.

By natural laws we mean such as God has ordained for the conservation and promotion of bodily health and strength, which are manifestly of primary importance, our bodies being the habitations of our spirits (1 Cor. 3: 16; 6: 19, 20), and upon their well-being depending our capacities for activity and enjoyment in this world. Hence, as instructed by the Christ, the first practical duty and work of his disciples being to heal the physically sick and infirm (Matt. 10: 1, 8), so manifestly this should be also the primary duty of the church. It is a great error—equivalent in fact to deferring our social salvation wholly to the next life—to suppose the culture of true religion does not include the culture of bodily health, and the prevention and cure of all its diseases and infirmities. All the prophets, the Christ himself, and all his apostles, thus interpret his mission (Ps. 103: 3; Ezek. 34: 4; Mal. 4: 2; Matt. 4: 23; Luke 9: 6, 11). In fact, it would be impossible to have any practical conception of the forgiveness of sins, unless such absolution were evidenced of its healing power—all diseases and infirmities having resulted from our transgressions of God's laws (Mark 2: 10, 11). Hence natural laws, so far as they pertain to the promotion and preservation of health, should be so thoroughly taught in our public schools that all persons will be without excuse for the violation thereof. And to the end that they may be enforced, every citizen should be provided with ample space and opportunity for the free exercise of his body and mind, pure air, water and sunlight, comfortable clothing and shelter. All dwellings and business houses should be so constructed and apart from each other as to permit of proper ventilation and drainage. Unclean habits, pollutions, adulterations, extravagances, and excesses of any kind should be strictly prohibited.

Moreover, that the sins of parents may not be visited upon their children, no persons should be permitted to marry who are incapable of producing reasonably healthy offspring. Nor should those who do marry be permitted to live and rear their children in other than healthy conditions and surroundings.

What is true of natural is true also of moral laws—written on tables of stone by the finger of God, and therefore immutable and imperishable, to which we must conform our political polities, if ever the world be redeemed and saved, and liberty, equality, and fraternity, practically realized ; and as these when fulfilled in love develop into the gospel of the Christ— and there could be no gospel except by such fulfillment—it is the duty of every Christian as a citizen of the world to apply his faith to their enforcement both in letter and spirit.

Now as parents are permitted to rule their children solely for their good, and have no disciplinary authority over them except to compel them to do what is essential to their well-being, or to refrain from doing what is detrimental thereto, so is the government permitted to rule and discipline its people. And as the family is a community in which parents and children share equitably in all possessions and privileges, so is the State a coöperative association, a commonwealth, established for the promotion of just and equitable social relations and interests. Deriving its authority wholly from God the Father, it is wholly paternal, as the relations of individuals to each other—all being children of God—are fraternal. And whether it be vested in a judge, king, or president, it is absolute so far as it fulfills its divine purpose, and does nothing more or less than to enforce the moral law both in letter and spirit. It must represent and enforce the will of God, not the personal will of the ruler any farther than he is himself just, nor the will of the people governed except to the degree they are disposed to love God and each other. "He hath showed thee, O man, what is good; and what doth the Lord require of thee but to do justly, and to love mercy, and to walk humbly with thy God?" (Mic. 6: 8). As liberty is attainable only through voluntary obedience to the laws of God, self-government —which is freedom—is permissible only to the degree no government at all is required. Otherwise self-government is mob-law. Whatever then is for the common good of the community the government has not only a right, but is also required, to do or forbid to be done; and as it represents the power and will of the supreme Father, all individual interests must be subordinate thereto. And as earth, air, water, and light are the natural gifts of God bestowed upon all men, whether just or unjust (Matt. 5: 45), the titles thereto are mediately vested in the government, that the use thereof may be apportioned equally among all people as they have need. Nothing, in fact, can be justly claimed by any individual as exclusively his own, except what he has himself created or earned by his own industry ; and as all men are social beings, even that which is one's own must be held for the common good.

Now while the constitutions and laws of Christian nations are for the most part fairly just so far as they go, and in conformity with natural and moral laws of God, yet, being self-ishly interpreted and administered in the letter only, they have become exceedingly unjust and oppressive. Hence Christian faith should be applied not so much for the repeal thereof as for such modification and improvement as will secure their practical administration in the spirit. And to this end every constitution should contain a preamble or declaration of principles, affirming that the purpose of the government is to enforce the will of God from whom all authority is derived:—that natural laws as defined in his Book of Nature, and moral laws as defined in his written Word are the full and perfect symbols thereof; and that no legislation shall be deemed lawful that is not in harmony therewith both in letter and spirit. With such declaration no executive officer, legislature, or judge can rightly enforce, make, or construe any civil law otherwise than in the spirit of the gospel of liberty, equality, and fraternity. Thus, if all avarice and selfishness be interpreted by the courts as thievery, and all social tyranny, oppression, and hatred as murder, as they really are (1 John 3 : 15), there will be no difficulty in the solution of social problems. A true government possessing, as it does, all the authority of the infinite Father in the enforcement of his Will, is practically a court of equity to which all persons can appeal for the redress of their grievances, and it has a right, and is required, to protect all its people in all natural and lawfully acquired rights.

PART II.

"Look on us,"—so said Peter and John to this beggar. Although they had stopped and fastened their eyes upon him, it is not likely that his attention had been specially attracted to them among the multitude who were thronging in at the gate, some of whom had no doubt stopped long enough to bestow alms upon him. But aroused by these earnest words he looked up, and beheld two men—strangers, but whose profound interest in him, and sympathy in his distress, were unmistakable. Naturally he gave heed unto them, expecting to receive something from them ; and though at first he may have anticipated nothing better than money, confidence was inspired in his breast that they were his friends, and were willing and able to help him. The tone of voice with which they bade him look on them, and the expression of their eyes so intently fixed upon him, permitted of no doubt of this. And when we reflect that they were the immediate disciples of the Christ,

281

had forsaken all to follow their Master, were
one with their Master in Spirit and purpose,
and endowed with his miraculous gifts, we cannot wonder that such tone and expression
should have imparted to this poor cripple a
miraculous inspiration, put into his feet and
ankle bones strength, made a new man of him,
and given him power when bidden to leap and
walk. Never before had he beheld fixed upon
him, the eyes of pure unselfishness and at the
same time of a faith able to remove mountains.
Nor can we doubt that could the poor and oppressed in our day, when we, who profess to be
ministers of Christ, as Peter and John were,
fasten our eyes upon them, see therein a like
expression of unselfish love, and a like consciousness of divine power, miracles of redemption might be wrought in their behalf. Not that
we do not wish to do our duty, but that our
sense of duty has become so dulled by the
stress of our private and temporal necessities,
arising from the unnatural and oppressive social conditions in which we are involved, and
by which we seem compelled to live for bread
alone, so limited to the perfunctory discharge
of conventional obligations that we have ourselves become spiritually crippled, and our
sacred calling perverted into a system of pro-

fessioual beggary. Not that we do not stop when we hear cries of distress, and fix our eyes upon those who utter them, but that our attitude is so conventional and patronizing that, so far from inspiring the poor with self-respect and personal aspirations and efforts for improvement, we arouse in their breasts feelings of resentment and envy. Not that we have no faith, but that we are so dependent on the rich for our support, and are ourselves so worldminded, that we "have the faith of our Master in respect of persons," and are incapable of working miracles or inspiring any practical hope of redemption. Not that we have no charitable feeling, but that we have ourselves become so dependent upon the charities of the rich, we have come to think that the gifts of God may be purchased with money, and that alms-giving—the distribution of the crumbs which fall from the rich men's tables (Luke 16: 21)—is the best that can be done for the poor.

As God, through the lips of his prophets of old, exhorted all men to look unto him and be saved (Isa. 45: 22), and in these last days has spoken by his Son (Heb. 1: 1, 2), saying, "Come unto me all ye that labor and are heavy laden, and I will give you rest" (Matt. 11: 28), so also Peter and John, apostles and ministers

of the Christ, recognizing in this helpless, hopeless despised human being a brother man, exhorted him to look on them. As their spirit
and purpose were inspired of their Master, they
were in the place of their Master, as their Master was in the place of God, and to look on
them was practically to look on their Master
and their God. What God and the Son of
God were to them, such were they to this
beggar—their eyes God's unselfish eyes, and
their voice God's unselfish voice; and such too
are all true ministers of Christ to all who labor
and are heavy laden.

Believing the Christ in the flesh to have been
the revelation of what God in the spirit is in
his relations to men, and that the Church he
established here is his constant and visible
presence in the world, we cannot doubt that,
if the hope and effort of the gospel for our
social redemption were responded to, as this
hitherto helpless and hopeless man responded
to the exhortation of Peter and John, in corresponding hope and effort on the part of all
or any who by the sin and selfishness of the
world are deprived of their natural and just
rights, the whole power of God would be exerted for their justification. Indeed this is as
certainly true as that there is an infinite and

supreme Power, Love, and Mercy, and that his Way, Truth, and Life are revealed and illustrated in Perfect Man.

Assuming, therefore, that the motive of Peter and John, when they exhorted this human moth to look on them, was to awaken such hope of redemption in his breast as would inspire him with corresponding effort to realize it, we ought not to doubt that, to the degree the church inspires a like hope, it may without hypocrisy, and with the consciousness of limitless power in God, exhort all men to look unto itself and be saved; for as through sin and selfishness all suffering and injustice are evolved and developed in society, there is a reasonable hope of redemption—nay, an absolute certainty thereof —presented in the true Church of Christ, from which sin and selfishness are excluded. But if the poor and oppressed hear in the voice of the congregation, or see in its eyes, the expression only of worldly pride, vanity, haughty condescension, or pharisaical self-righteousness, it is impossible that it should possess any power of God, or inspire any reasonable hope of redemption either in this life or in the life to come, however devout its attitude may otherwise be, or frequent its prayers. Surely the crippled and enslaved classes of society—crippled and enslaved by poverty, by infirmities of body and mind, degraded and brutalized by constant and excessive toil, rusted and dissipated by idleness or useless luxuries, or depraved and vitiated by violations of natural and moral laws,—can be inspired with no earnest and practical efforts for self-improvement by looking upon world-minded congregations, dainty priests, stately bishops, frantic exhorters, dogmatic schoolmen, ritualistic novelties, vain austerities, affected pietisms, magical infusions of holiness, juggleries, incantations, and fetichisms. Not that our church membership is composed wholly or mostly of willful hypocrites, but that, blinded and deceived by mere conventional forms of godliness, which have no power thereof (2 Tim. 3: 5), and carried away by zeal without knowledge (Rom. 10: 2)—a sectarian, consuming and wasting zeal (Ps. 69: 9; John 2: 17)—most members have become unconscious of what the mission of the Christ really was. What can be more unreasonable, not to say hypocritical, than for us to exhort sinners to look unto us and be clean, when we ourselves are but whited sepulchres full of all uncleanness?—to be at peace with God and men, when we are full of sectarian and dogmatic strife?—to renounce the world, when we are as worldly as the world itself? What do we mean when we exhort sinners to come into the church and be saved? What is it to be saved, and what is there in our congregations that inspires a reasonable hope of salvation? Surely nothing, except it be the practical realization therein of Fatherhood in God and Sonship and Brotherhood in Christ.

No doubt, as Christian hope is the natural evolution of Christian faith (2 Cor. 10: 15; Heb. 11: 1), and must correspond therewith in spirit and purpose, the unreasonableness of that now presented in the congregations of the church has resulted from a corresponding weakness and inefficiency of their faith, largely corrupted from a belief and trust in the Fatherhood of God to a belief and trust in creeds, statutes, and ordinances of man's appointment, and applied to sensual, superstitious, and sectarian uses. Manifestly there is no inspiring hope developed from such creeds, statutes, and ordinances. They are but contentions with the Almighty, instructing and reproving God (Job 40: 2), condemning him that we may be righteous (Job 40: 2, 8),—not wrath against injustice, nor looking on the proud to condemn and abase them (Job 40: 11, 12) whereby we are saved by our own right hand (14),—but attempts of

selfish men to subdue and limit God's great
power in the Church with lines, hooks, and
thorns (Job 41: 1, 2). They represent only
the hypocrite's hope (Job 27: 8), for there can
be no greater hypocrisy than to attempt to develop Christian hope from faith in creeds, statutes, and ordinance of man's appointment—
nay, to affirm and enforce them upon the human
conscience and reason—thus asserting salvation
in the name of men, when we are expressly told
that there is no other name under heaven given
among men but that of Jesus Christ of Nazareth whereby they must be saved.   Not till we
present a reasonable way in which the prison
doors of social oppression and repression can be
opened, and all infirmity and distress removed
—which was the mission of the Christ—can we
develop a reasonable hope of salvation.

Moreover the hope now presented by the
churches is unreasonable, because its realization is almost wholly deferred to the future life
—not necessarily, for we can, if we will, do
God's will on earth as it is done in heaven;
can treat each other in the church as the children of God treat each other in heaven—but
because we are unwilling to dwell together as
brethren and members of the household of God,
sharing justly with each other in our burdens

and privileges, our sorrows and joys. How can we reasonably exhort men to lay up their treasures in heaven, when we ourselves are laying up our treasures on earth to be corrupted by moths and rust, or stolen by thieves? How indeed can our earthly treasures be laid up in heaven and become imperishable,—we having brought nothing into this world, and it being certain we can carry nothing out (1 Tim. 6: 7)—except we devote them to the interests of the church, which, if the true church, is heaven on earth? to defer to the morrow what can be done to-day (Prov. 3: 28; Matt. 6: 34; Jas. 4: 13–17)— the realization of hopes and the enjoyment of treasures which may be in a measure realized and enjoyed now,—is but to disappoint our hopes and waste our treasures; and the motive of such procrastination is either selfish and worldly, or must spring from our own lack of faith in the power of God to help and save us, and therefore is hypocritical—unlike that which inspired the Psalmist's prayer: "Save *now*, I beseech thee, O Lord; O Lord, I beseech thee, send *now* prosperity" (Ps. 118: 25).

As we enter the church that we may save our souls, which are our greatest treasures, so should we bring with us into the church all other treasures that they too may be saved,—

nay, must bring them with us if we save them
at all, for there is no way to save anything but
by using it for the purpose God designed it to
be used.   In no instance did the Christ defer
the practical realization of the hopes he inspired
to the next life.   He did not say to the lame,
blind, deaf, leprous, possessed of devils or otherwise oppressed, Wait till you die; and then I
will heal your infirmities, and release you from
your thralldom, but to all who believed in him,
and responded to the hope of salvation presented in his gospel with personal efforts to help
themselves, he restored strength and health,
cast out their devils, forgave their sins, re-
mitted their penalties, and set them at liberty.
Not that final and complete exaltation and
freedom can be attained immediately in a sinful and selfish world, any more than a babe
can become instantly a man, but that it can be
begun at once, assured and partially realized,—
howbeit the disciple cannot be above his Master,
but must be as his Master ; and though he be
subject as was his Master to temptation, and
death, he will like him be made perfect through
suffering, raised up, and glorified (Rev. 2: 10).
No congregation can be faithful unto death,
except it strive to live here as they live in
heaven—doing the will of God here as it is

done in heaven, and realizing the hopes and promises of the gospel here as they are realized in heaven.

Wherefore Peter and John, apostles and ministers of the Christ—sent into the world by him even as he was sent—sought to apply their hope to the immediate redemption of all men, to heal every infirmity, right every wrong, and open every prison door. They were prepared to say to this beggar that right there and then he might practically realize the hope and promise of the gospel of Jesus Christ of Nazareth. And certainly, to be able to rise and walk and enter within the Beautiful Gate was to realize such hope and promise so far as this earthly life is concerned. Being enabled to walk, admitted to a congregation in which all were brethren, each doing unto others as he would they should do unto him, it was impossible that he should be compelled longer to beg his bread, or come short of any gift of God. Hence we may assert with entire confidence that, so far as the Church does not seek to shirk, postpone and avoid its responsibilities, but is willing now and here to take any man by the hand, however poor and despised, who through faith is willing to make proper effort to help himself, set him on his feet, bring him

into the Fold of the Good Shepherd, and share
equally with him as he has need of all its privileges and possessions, it will to the full measure of its faith be endowed with the power of
God to redeem lost souls—"to loose the bands
of wickedness, to undo the heavy burdens, and
to let the oppressed go free;" nay, even to forgive sins (Matt. 9: 6; 2 Cor. 2: 10), and raise
the dead to life (Col. 3: 1-4). To the degree
only that we make effort to undo the heavy
burdens of others, to open every prison door,
and to break every yoke of oppression, can we
inspire reasonable hope, or possess power to
forgive or be forgiven (Luke 1: 17; John 20:
23). In no instance did the Christ pronounce
remission of sins without removing the burdens
and penalties which were incurred by sin
(Matt. 9: 2, 5, 6). So also the proper and only
practical way to raise the dead to life, or to become ourselves partakers of the resurrection, is
to impart such hope to the hopeless, and such
life to the dead in trespass and sins—and there
is really no other death—as will quicken them
to a new life, and inspire them with efforts and
aspirations for self-improvement (Jas. 5: 15).

We cannot impart to others what we do not
ourselves possess; and no professed minister of
Christ possesses a reasonable hope, unless he be

willing to follow his Master's example of personal self-denial and self-sacrifice for the salvation of men—to give, as he has received, opportunities to others equal as with what he himself possesses. Manifestly, if we have not been quickened by the inspiring hope of the gospel, we cannot quicken others,—if not ourselves forgiven our debts, cannot forgive others their debts,—if not risen with Christ from the dead, cannot raise others from the dead (Col. 3: 1). In fact, unless we be already risen in Christ, when our dust is returned to dust, there is no promise of resurrection thereafter. By seeking in this life "the things which are above" are we prepared to realize them in the next life— loving our neighbor as ourself, making him rich as we are rich, sharing his burdens, healing his infirmities, making him free as we are free, and leading him in with us at the Beautiful Gate to a social condition in which "there shall be no more death, sorrow, nor crying." Indeed a reasonable hope, whereby we are quickened, and inspired with aspirations and efforts for the improvement of our social condition, is itself resurrection to a new life (Col. 2: 12).

Every true hope is manifestly one which, when realized, confers a blessing. Hence, to apply our hope practically is to strive to bestow

blessings upon our fellow-men. Every beati-
tude of the gospel of the Christ is one of hope,
and is partially realized by every true disciple
here in this life.   Thus the Christ did not say,
Blessed *will be* the poor in spirit, for theirs *will
be* the Kingdom of Heaven in the next life, but,
"Blessed *are* the poor in spirit, for theirs *is* the
Kingdom of Heaven"—both here and here-
after.   No person can enter the true church except he be poor in spirit, however rich in purse
—conscious that through sin and selfishness he
is poor and blind and miserable, and through
repentance led to seek the reformation and improvement of his condition,—but if permitted
to enter, each member being as rich as the combined riches of all members, he is no longer
poor in this life, and being moreover a son of
God and member of his household, he is a joint
heir with Christ in the boundless riches of the
heavenly kingdom (Rom. 8: 17; 1 Tim. 6: 17).

To impart therefore, to the poor and oppressed in this life the hope, opportunity, and
privilege of becoming members of the Church
of Christ is the greatest blessing possible for us
to bestow; and certainly we can do this if the
congregation represents a real brotherhood, in
which no man calls aught of the things he possesses his own, and all things are common.   In

this way can we truthfully and practically say
unto those who mourn, Ye shall be comforted;
—to the meek, Ye shall inherit the earth;—to
the hungry and athirst after righteousness, Ye
shall be filled;—to the merciful, Ye shall obtain
mercy;—to the pure, Ye shall see God;—to the
peacemakers, Ye shall be called the children of
God;—to those who are persecuted for righteousness' sake, Yours is the Kingdom of God;
—to those who die in the Lord, Your works
shall follow you. But if neither the poor and
miserable nor the rich and selfish will repent
and respond to the saving faith and hope we
seek to impart, when we stop and fix our eyes
upon them, with efforts to help themselves, we,
as Christians, can only weep for them as the
Christ wept over Jerusalem (Luke 19: 41, 42),
and the great prophet of Israel wept over his
people (Jer. 9: 1–6)—howbeit, as citizens of the
State, we may and should still strive, through
the discipline of the law, to bring them to
Christ.

But manifestly Christian hope is not only objective, not simply the desire and promise of
realizing outward things, but also subjective,
that which hungers and thirsts after righteousness, whereby it may attain to the inward realization of redeemed and ennobled manhood,—

for "what shall it profit a man if he shall gain the whole world, and lose his own soul" (Mark 8: 36)—be accorded all social rights, privileges, and possessions that can be objectively realized in this earthly life, and yet, from lack of spiritual culture, ultimately find the Beautiful Gate closed and bolted against him? This, however is really an absurd hypothesis, since it is manifestly impossible for any man to improve or possess anything at all except to the degree of his spiritual development and consciousness, from which he derives all his capacities for enjoyment. Indeed all ideas of liberty, equality, and fraternity are but idle dreamings, utterly fanciful and impractical, if not inspired with heavenly aspirations through the Spirit of Truth, Justice, and Love. To possess any good gift is not to possess it—is really poverty, misery, and shame—if we do not appreciate its value, or if we pervert it to unnatural uses. Thus money hoarded, or spent in riotous living, is not riches but a source of poverty to its possessor. To hope for liberty without the culture of obedience, or for equality without the culture of personal nobility of character, or for fraternity without mutual love, is not only absurd, but can result only in confusion and shame. Christian "hope maketh not ashamed, because the love of God is shed abroad in our hearts by the Holy Spirit which is given unto us " (Rom. 5: 5). And without such love no practicable and just system of sociology can be devised, nor indeed any human being redeemed from social bondage to the world, the flesh, and the devil.

Had this beggar's hope been simply to receive some objective thing of Peter and John, or had he been content with such gift as he at first desired, aspiring for nothing better—nothing that would have ennobled his personal character, and developed a consciousness of true self-respect, manliness, and independence —he would have remained a beggar, and his hope would have made him ashamed; for every man is a beggar and destitute of true self-respect, however poor or rich in outward things, who is willing to subsist upon the fruits of other men's labors. Hence, if any men or class of men, either by legalized or revolutionary methods, being themselves poor in purse, seek to compel others rich in purse to share their riches with them; or being rich in purse, avail themselves of their riches to compel the poor to support them in idleness and useless luxuries and extravagances, they are beggars, and their inspiring motive or hope will inevitably make them ashamed. Mutual dependence, however, whereby we give as we receive according to our abilities and necessities, doing unto others as we would they should do unto us—helping each other as we receive help from the Father of all, —is social freedom, our hopes being inspired by motives of brotherly kindness and love.

When, therefore, we seek to apply our Christian hope to the discipline of the world that it may be brought to Christ, we should strive to establish and enforce such statutes and ordinances as will confer upon all individuals equal opportunities of helping themselves, while at the same time all are required to help each other. This may seem contradictory and absurd—that the opportunity of helping one's self should be conferred only on condition that we help each other; for if one needs help to help himself he would seem to be in no condition to help others. But every helper needs help, even as Peter and John needed the help of God to work this miracle, and needed also the help of this beggar in their ministry, that the glory of God might be made manifest in him (John 9: 2, 3). Nay, even God and his Christ need help—the coöperation of all sinful men—that the world may be redeemed. Helping others is, therefore, helping

ourselves; and helping ourselves is helping
others. And manifestly the first requisite to
mutual help is that every person should possess
every needful opportunity of helping himself
that he may be able to help others. Indeed
there can be no reasonable hope developed of
our faith except to the degree that opportunity
of realizing such hope be first developed. That
is, next to faith, opportunity is the primary requisite of hope; and in order to apply our hope
to the redemption of the world, we must endeavor as citizens of the world to secure to
each individual the opportunity of self-support,
and of limitlessly improving his social condition.

But while it is easy to say and understand
that the primary requisite to the practical application of Christian hope to the redemption
of the world from social thralldom is that every
person be given ample opportunity for improvement, it is confessedly very difficult to confer
such opportunity—not, however, that the way
is not plain, but that many are either too selfish
to pursue it, too spiritually blind and ignorant
to discern it, or so hopelessly discouraged, depraved, indolent, or thriftless, that they are indisposed to seek or improve opportunities when
conferred upon them. Hence ample opportu-

nities should not only be conferred upon all individuals and classes of society, so that none will have any excuse for beggary, rust, or thievery, or any occasion for grievance, but all should also be compelled to improve them. Thus it is certainly practicable for the State to establish a public and free system of compulsory education, whereby to the utmost limits of their capabilities and desires all persons are enabled to acquire useful knowledge both theoretical and practical. And that they may have leisure for study, as also for such rest and recreation as are essential to health and happiness, the hours devoted to what is called business should, and no doubt can be, limited to such only as are requisite to the production of all things that are essential to the existence, well-being, and improvement of society. Doubtless if all persons who are capable of labor were required to work for their living, three or four hours daily devoted thereto would be sufficient to supply all necessities,—all moths, rust, and thieves being eliminated, as they easily could, be, if all members of society were granted equal opportunities, and all consumers were compelled to be producers. Nor is such legislation impracticable, but is an imperative duty on the part of the government, and should be immediately enacted and enforced—quite as imperative as is the duty of every parent to educate and discipline his children for future usefulness. To be sure, very much "business" would by such legislation be suppressed, and also much that is called "business enterprise," but is only avarice, and without true hope or aspiration for improvement. With less business and more laborers the burdens of the people would be correspondingly lightened. In this simple way all labor problems would be solved. And doubtless, all nations professedly Christian are already so leavened with the spirit of the gospel, as to render such legislation as will confer upon all good citizens equal opportunities for increase and improvement not only wise and practicable, but also absolutely essential to their own safety and permanence.

But when we say such legislation should be immediately enacted and enforced, we do not mean that much patience is not requisite thereto; for in the nature of things no hopes can be realized in an instant of time any more than the hope in the seed can at once be realized in the full corn in the ear. Indeed nothing good can be realized until we have first acquired patience, to wait for it—(Luke 8 : 15; Rom. 5 : 3, 4; Col. 1 : 11; Heb. 6 : 12; Jas. 1 : 3, 4; 5 : 7;

Rev. 3 : 10); for otherwise by undue haste we should not only disappoint our hopes, but also subject ourselves to greater evils. "Sufficient unto the day is the evil thereof" (Matt. 6: 33, 34; 2 Cor. 12: 9, 10), howbeit we should never be content in social bondage, or willingly suffer wrong. Patience is not content, but is persistence in well-doing, and fortitude to endure all things essential to the ultimate realization of our hopes. We cannot reform the government by overthrowing it by revolutionary methods, whereby we destroy the power of just legislation whereon our hope of political freedom is based. "It is useless to kick against the pricks," and unwise to kill the goose which lays the golden eggs.

To be sure, it is better voluntarily to obey the laws of God—in which case there would be no necessity of any civil government,—but such freedom can only be fully realized when all men become members of the true church of Christ. Of course, hope alone is not realization, howbeit it is the forerunner and medium thereof, and as such is a foretaste of the freedom and joy which such realization brings.

While, therefore, we are not permitted to resort to unnatural and unlawful methods to obtain our object, and it will require time to secure the requisite legislation, yet as the men who labor and are heavy laden vastly outnumber the parasites who subsist upon the fruits of their labors, there is no doubt at all that they can without unreasonable delay secure the enactment and enforcement of such statutes and ordinances as will confer equal opportunities upon all, and at the same time compel all, according to their abilities, to pursue useful occupations and contribute equally to the common necessities of life. And to this end all injurious or useless occupations, all dissipations, monopolies, or combinations whereby one class seeks to promote its selfish interests to the detriment of another's, and all other parasitic evils resulting from violations either in the letter or spirit of the natural or moral laws should be rigidly suppressed. In this way all selfishness or pseudo-respectability that boasts itself in and defends its ill-gotten gains by the law, will be overcome by the law, and made to appear criminal as it really is. So also, as avarice is thereby repressed, the vast concentrations of wealth in the hands of a few will in like degree be repressed, while at the same time the aggregate of wealth in the community will be correspondingly increased and distributed.

And finally, that the State may really and practically become a commonwealth, and may possess the means and power of conferring upon all good citizens equal privileges and opportunities, it should, in the exercise of its undoubted rights of eminent domain, decree that all titles to earth, air, water, sunshine, and all other free gifts of God not already alienated, be inalienably vested in Itself for the equitable use of all good citizens. And further, that at the death of each citizen all his titles to property of any public value—real, personal, and mixed,—shall also become vested in the State ; howbeit, that so long as an individual lives, and is obedient to the laws, he be permitted to honestly create, acquire, possess, and enjoy all personal properties to the utmost limits of his abilities and desires.

Thus, and without trespassing upon the rights of any, all citizens would be permitted to hope for limitless improvements, and none would lack ample opportunities for the practical realization thereof.

PART III.

APPLIED CHARITY.

"SILVER and gold have I none," said Peter to this beggar who, when bidden, had looked wistfully into the Apostles' faces, expecting to receive something from them. As he had asked an alms, and never had hoped for anything better—his infirmity being deemed incurable from birth—he doubtless would have been grateful and content according to the measure of his expectations, had they each bestowed on him a penny. Most beggars are satisfied with the gift of money, and most persons who bestow it upon them, finding them content therewith, are also satisfied that they have done the best they could to help the poor, and to fulfill the requirements of the gospel of charity. That is, money has come to be regarded, both in the world and in the church, as the greatest blessing we can bestow or receive, whereas it is intrinsically of little value or necessity—none at all, in fact, except to the degree it has become a necessity through our cupidity and

305

selfishness, whereby we are unwilling to bestow upon each other what we need without money or price. Indeed we are expressly told that it cannot purchase the gifts of God (2 Kings 5: 16; Isa. 55: 1; Acts 8: 20); and our Lord forbade his disciples to use it, or even take it with them, in their ministrations, when he sent them out into the world to proclaim his gospel—although they used it as citizens of the world to purchase what was essential to physical sustenance, and to pay taxes to Cæsar (Matt. 17: 24-27; John 4: 8). Nor is it likely that Peter and John would have bestowed any alms upon this beggar had their pockets been full of silver and gold, for the simple reason that they had something better to give. Yet, had they had nothing but money, they doubtless would, as the Scribes and Pharisees doubtless did, have tossed into his lap a penny or two as they passed him by. In fact we may assert positively, from the letter and spirit of the gospel, that the more we rely upon a moneyed charity, the greater will be the necessity thereof; and on the other hand, the more brotherly kindness and love are cultivated— which is real and genuine charity—the less occasion will there be for the use of money. For to the degree we love God and our fellow-men will we share with each other whatever we possess without money or price (Isa. 55: 1; Matt. 13: 46; 14: 15-22; 1 Cor. 9: 13, 14). As the law is bondage, and money is a creature of the law, we cannot by the use of money satisfy the requirements of love, or ourselves be delivered from the bondage of the law into the glorious liberty of the children of God.

If, therefore, we be ministers of Christ—having, as we profess to have, something to bestow upon the poor better than money,—we should not give money, but that which is better, else our righteousness would not exceed that of the Scribes and Pharisees and we could in no case enter into the kingdom of heaven (Matt. 5: 20).

Evidently there must be something better than alms, and if there be, alms is not charity; for charity is love, which is better than anything else, a pure unselfishness; and without love nothing is of any more value than a barren fig tree. Even faith and hope are fruitless if they do not evolve love; for "though I have all faith so that I could remove mountains, and have not charity, I am nothing; and though I bestow all my goods to feed the poor, and though I give my body to be burned, and have not charity, it profiteth me nothing" (1 Cor. 13: 2, 3). Not that faith, or alms, or martyr-

dom can have no merit, but that, except to the
degree the motive thereof is unselfish love, it is
like the good seed sown by the wayside, or on
stony ground, or among thorns, and brings no
fruit to perfection. The like is true of the
law, if it be not fulfilled in love. Not that the
law is sin, it being a necessary discipline for the
suppression of selfishness, and to lead us to repentance, but that "if righteousness come by
the law Christ is dead in vain" (Gal. 2: 21).

Alms-giving, therefore,—though essential as
a discipline under the law, and no person can
become a Christian except he be willing to give
unto others as he would that others should give
unto him, is not Christianity—Christianity requiring us to give freely without thought of
return, and even when we know there can be
no return. Alms-giving is good citizenship in
the world, and as such is a social duty, but is
not the end of the law for righteousness to
every or any one that believeth (Rom. 10: 4),
and if relied upon as such renders us unrighteous. Plainly, therefore, no man can be a true
follower of Christ, or member of his church,
except to the degree the motive of his faith and
hope be unselfish love of God and Man. And
if simple alms-giving be not such love, he must,
like Peter and John, in order to become a

Christian, have something of more value to give than silver and gold. Otherwise he might have nothing at all to give, and others, less loving than he, have much, the value and amount of charity being estimated by a standard of silver or gold.

Being simply the fruit of secular labors, money can be of no intrinsic value except to promote secular interests; and if we regard, use, receive, and bestow it as the end of the law for righteousness, we show plainly that the religion we profess has become secularized, practiced only in the letter, and that we ourselves are mercenary in spirit. What then? Is alms-giving a sin? God forbid; for as the law was added because of our transgressions (Gal. 3: 19), and its penalties inflicted as a necessary discipline to bring us to repentance, whereby it might be fulfilled in love, so alms-giving is ordained because of our selfishness, and is essential to the restraint and discipline of our cupidity. And as we, as citizens of the world, subject to Cæsar, must obey the law, so must we, when required, give alms to the poor to supply their temporal necessities. But in the church, in which all are citizens of the heavenly kingdom, and equal with each other (Gal. 3: 28),— for all members are one body in Christ, and whether one member suffer, all members suffer with it (1 Cor. 12: 25-27)—there is no occasion for alms-giving any more than in a private family, in which parents and children share equally with each other in all their possessions. If, therefore, one member gives money as alms to another he is not a true member, not apprehending what the spirit of the church or of true charity is.

As the true Christian fulfills the law in love, —that is, because he loves justice and honesty, —so does he give to the church, sharing equally with his fellow-members all his possessions, not grudgingly or of necessity, but cheerfully (2 Cor. 9: 7) through love of God and his fellow-men—not by compulsion, or as a duty or debt. Nor does any member receive free gifts of his fellow-members, or of God, as a beggar receives them, but because he is a free man, needs them, has a right to them, and knows they are freely given for the love of giving. Alms-giving at the best is only the testimony of a pitiful feeling which, though it be a credit to us, is not charity: for we may give all our goods to feed the poor through our pity for their suffering, and yet not love them unselfishly. In fact it is degrading, and should make us ashamed to permit ourselves either to become an object of pity, or to bestow gifts through a feeling of pity only. In other words, except pity develop into love, it is but as sounding brass or tinkling cymbal.

To interpret charity practically as alms, and limiting its idea thereto, is as erroneous as practically to interpret Christianity as simply obedience to the moral law in the letter. To be sure, we cannot be Christians except we give alms and obey the moral law in the letter, yet are we not Christians till alms-giving and the law are fulfilled in spirit—that is, voluntarily, through love of God and our brother men. Otherwise, if not bestowed in love—alms serve to vitiate the motive not only of those who bestow them, but also of those who receive them, rendering it selfish and mercenary, and, so far from alleviating poverty and distress, tends to aggravate and increase them. On the one hand, it is simply an effort to purchase salvation with money, and on the other betrays a willingness to repress,—as Esau did when he sold his birthright for a mess of pottage—one's natural aspirations for freedom, and his personal sense of manliness and self-respect, for a mere pittance grudgingly bestowed. Indeed there can be no pure charity bestowed through a sense of duty, debt, moral obligation, or personal gain, but

only through unselfish love of God and Man;
nor can any be received except as a natural
right, or as purchased without money or price,
—although all social duties, debts, and moral
obligations must be enforced and discharged
until the law be fulfilled in love.

The mission of the Christ was not to collect
alms and distribute them among the poor, for
that could be and was done before his coming,
and he had a much greater and better work to
accomplish—to fulfill the law in love, whereby
the necessity of alms would be done away.
Nor is this the mission of the Church, it not
being an eleemosynary institution—hospital,
poorhouse, insane asylum, or other infirmary,—
but the Kingdom of God, in which there are no
moths, rusts, or thieves.   That is, it solves all
social problems of poverty, dissipation, and
thievery, not by alms-giving, but by making its
members free and equal, and conferring upon
them unlimited opportunities of acquiring all
true riches.   Hence it is not the mission of
either clergy or laity, as such, to collect and
distribute alms; nor should the church build
"institutions of charity," so called, thus assuming the burdens which God has imposed upon
the world as a necessary and just discipline—
really condoning the sin and selfishness of the

world, whereby all its social oppressions and sufferings have been justly imposed upon it, and encouraging it to go on in sin and selfishness that righteousness and charity may abound. Manifestly the redemption of the world cannot be secured in this way, any more than Peter and John could have redeemed this beggar by tossing him a penny.

Doubtless nothing has tended more to the corruption and demoralization of the congregations of the churches than almsgiving—the clergy having become professional beggars by devoting their time chiefly to collecting and distributing money for so-called charitable purposes, and the laity becoming blinded thereby to real charity, as were the Pharisees, who deemed themselves righteous because they gave tithes of all they possessed (Luke 18 : 12), yet binding heavy burdens and grievous to be borne on men's shoulders, which they were unwilling to move with one of their fingers (Matt. 23 : 4). Indeed, while we have been extremely zealous in collecting and distributing alms, we have been strangely oblivious of the burdens, grievous and hard to be borne, that we bind on men's shoulders, which we have not striven to lift with one of our fingers. And those of us who are most indifferent to the oppressions of our fellow-men are often the most zealous in alms-giving—thereby, no doubt, flattering ourselves that our alms atone for our lack of real charity.

Charity, as St. Paul affirms, must begin at home; and if one gives alms abroad while his own household is suffering he is a hypocrite, his charity being such only in pretense. And if that person be a member of the church, he hath denied the faith, and is worse than an infidel (Gal. 6: 10; 1 Tim. 5: 8). And as we have shown that the mission of the church is not for the collection and distribution of alms, but to preach the gospel to the poor, to undo the heavy burdens, to open every prison door, and let the oppressed go free, we do not hesitate to affirm that taking up collections of any kind in the congregation for distribution of the common necessities of life outside the church is contrary to the spirit and purpose of the gospel—robbing the faithful to supply the necessities of the unfaithful. What advantage is a nominal membership in the church, if its organization does not secure to each and all members through mutual protection and support such competence in temporal necessities as the combined riches of all can afford? To promote a proper distribution of alms in the world we need only to go into politics, and as citizens of the world apply the principles of the gospel to secure all citizens in their natural rights, and make such provisions for the infirm as necessity may require. To the degree the congregation of the church impoverishes itself in order to relieve the world from its just burdens, it incapacitates itself for fulfilling its own mission, which is to furnish a refuge from the evils of the world, even as heaven above is a refuge. It is our ark of safety, the fold of the Good Shepherd, the shadow of a great Rock in a weary land, the Family and Household of God, in which no alms are collected.

Its members, however, are individually, as was their Master, sent into the world to bring lost sheep into the heavenly fold, that they may be saved from the persecutions, oppressions, and all other evils of the world—doing the same work the Christ did for the world, but not the work of the world. The world is not saved by easing it of its just burdens and penalties, for the gospel does not do away with the law, but by bringing sinners to repentance and into the fold of the Good Shepherd. Hence the parting instructions of the Christ to his disciples were, not to go out into the world to distribute the alms of the congregation among the poor, but to preach the gospel of repentance for the remission of sins, and by baptism to bring them in at the Beautiful Gate.

All public institutions and works for the relief of the poor that are of a temporal character and purpose only are of the law—that is of the civil government, which, if rightly constituted, derives its authority wholly from the principles of natural and moral law—and are no more of the church than are the courts of justice and prison houses erected for the prevention and punishment of vice and crime. The church distributes to the hungry not the bread Moses gave, but the Bread of Life that came down from heaven, which, if any man eat, he shall live forever (John 6 : 32–35)—although her members, being human beings, and subject to natural laws, need food, and should in natural and lawful ways earn their living, accumulate earthly riches, and share them equitably with each other according to their needs.

As the Church is an example to the world of the social polity of the Kingdom of God, of a purely unselfish social condition, and, though furnished with gates for protection against the world, was established in the world for the salvation of the world, she cannot fulfill her mission except she apply her charity thereto. In fact this is her mission, to redeem the world from all its social oppressions and sufferings; and except she strive to do this she perverts her mission to selfish purposes, and becomes the bulwark of social oppression. Hence her missionaries,—and all are missionaries—sent into the world to preach the gospel of glad tidings of obedience, peace, and brotherhood, must as citizens of the world become the social leaven of faith, hope, and charity therein—leaven hid in three measures of meal until the whole is leavened; grains of mustard seed growing into the greatest of all trees; treasures hid in the field; pearls of great price; nets cast into the sea (Matt. 13: 37-48). By becoming members and missionaries of the Church they do not cease to become citizens of the world, and except they make their Christian influence felt by applying their Christian principles to the utmost of their abilities in the world, they cease to be missionaries of the Church.

Now practically to apply our Christian charity in the world we should illustrate what Christian charity is in our personal and social relations with our fellow-men. We should strive to do better for them than they are doing for themselves; and though we as citizens give alms to relieve the immediate necessities of the poor, we should at the same time endeavor to

prevent the recurrence of such necessities
through our personal examples, and through
educational, business, and political agencies.
The mind should be in us " which was in Christ
Jesus, who being in the form of God thought
it not robbery to be equal with God, but made
himself of no reputation, and took upon him
the form of a servant, and was made in the
likeness of men ; and being found in fashion as
a man he humbled himself and became obedient unto death, even the death of the cross "
(Phil. 2: 5-8);—suffering persecution and
ignominy, yet overcoming evil with good;—
kind always, though suffering long; undergoing the discipline of the law, yet fulfilling the
same in love; tempted in all things as we are,
yet without sin. We should go out into the
world as he came into the world—cheerfully
denying ourselves as he denied himself, that we
may give the more. Nor should we, being in
the form of God as he was, think it robbery to
be equal with him ; that is, being his brethren,
and children together with him in our common
Father's household, and joint heirs with him in
his eternal inheritance, we should no longer regard ourselves as beggars, but as free and equal
in our participations in the boundless riches,
life, and glory of the Kingdom of God (Rom.

8: 15-19). Yet being imperfect after the fashion of sinful men, we must humble ourselves
that we may be exalted, seeking no earthly
reputation or recompense for our works of
charity, but making ourselves servants of men,
and unselfishly devoting our lives to their redemption and well-being.

With this lofty purpose, consciousness, and
self-respect which charity inspires, we can go
into the world and illustrate in our own lives
what true charity is, and inspire our fellow-
citizens with faith in God's power to right all
wrongs, and with Christian hope that maketh
not ashamed. Being ourselves charitable we
will not grudge, spite, or hate others who are
richer or otherwise more fortunate than we;
for "charity envieth not." Nor will we vainly
boast ourselves in our riches, righteousness, or
any superior gifts, honors, or personal endowments; for "charity vaunteth not itself, is not
puffed up." We will not be affected, ostenta-
tious, haughty, scornful, contemptuous, vulgar,
or otherwise disagreeable; for charity "doth
not behave itself unseemly." We will not be
ruled by selfish motives, or seek to promote our
own interests to the detriment of those of
others, covet another's possessions, or be un-
generous or unjust in our dealings; for charity

"seeketh not her own." Not quarrelsome, con-
tentious, resentful; for charity "is not easily
provoked." Not illiberal, cynical, austere,
prone to construe good as evil, or believe evil
reports, bigoted, harsh, unforgiving; for charity
" thinketh no evil." We will take no pleasure
in that others are worse than we (Luke 18: 11),
or in anything mean in ourselves, vicious, or
otherwise evil and debasing, or in social inequalities developed of selfishness, vanity, and
the pride of life, or in holding the truth in unrighteousness (Rom. 1: 18), in the deceivable-
ness of unrighteousness (2 Thess. 2: 10, 12);
for charity " rejoiceth not in iniquity, but rejoiceth in the truth," through love of the truth
—not rejecting it because it is unpopular or
contrary to our selfish interests (John 8: 40,
45), nor regarding those who tell us the truth
as our enemies, but as our friends (Gal. 4: 16).
We will bear all things—our own and others'
burdens (Rom. 15: 1, 2; Gal. 6: 2, 5); believe all things—that whatever ought to be will
be, and that truth, justice, and mercy are
always practical and expedient; hope all
things—confident that whatever ought to be,
whatever God has promised, and for which we
aspire in the Spirit of Truth, will surely come
to pass; endure all things—as well we may

through the power of Infinite Omnipotent Love, whereby all things are made to work for our good (Rom. 8 : 28), disciplines (Heb. 12 : 7), afflictions (2 Tim. 4 : 5), persecutions (1 Pet. 2 : 19), temptations (Jas. 1 : 12), contradictions (Heb. 12 : 2, 3), and even fools gladly, seeing we ourselves are wise (2 Cor. 11 : 19).

But as love and hate are necessarily involved, loving what is good being hating what is evil, and hating what is evil loving what is good (Ps. 97 : 10 ; Prov. 8 : 3 ; Eccl. 3 : 8 ; Matt. 6 : 24 ; 1 John 2 : 15), the degree of our power to love is always the measure of our power to hate, and our power to hate the measure of our power to love (Heb. 1 : 9). Thus we cannot feel love toward our enemies except we hate their malice, or for the sinner, except we loathe his sins. That is, the more our charity hates sin, the more will it strive to cleanse us and our fellow-men therefrom. Being practical and aggressive, it cannot be simply sentimental and passive.

Hence, while always loving, it never loves that which is neither lovable nor can be made lovable, but always loathes and hates it; while always liberal, it is never licentious, never indulges itself or others in indifference to duty, or in any dissipation or thriftlessness (Isa. 32 :

5, 6); while always kind, it is yet full of wrath
against all meanness, selfishness, injustice, and
cruelty (2 Sam. 12: 9, 10; Ps. 7: 11; Eph.
4: 26); while always pitiful and forgiving, it
never condones offences, or forgives the unre-
pentant or unforgiving (Matt. 6: 14, 15; 18:
32–35). While always helpful, it never helps
those who can but will not help themselves
(Mark 6: 5; Gal. 6: 7; 2 Thess. 3: 10); and
while always merciful, it is never unjust (Ps.
59: 5; Mich. 6: 8; Rom. 6: 12).

Such was the charity, better than silver and
gold, that Peter and John, as apostles and ministers of the Church, practically applied to the
redemption of this beggar. And the first
thing they did, after fixing their eyes on him
and bidding him look on them, was to take him
by the hand, thus condescending to one of low
estate (Rom. 12: 16)—not with pretentious
self-abasement, nor patronizingly, yet with the
manly consciousness of their superiority and
power in God, with unselfish desire to lift him
up to their own high level, and to confer upon
him equal opportunities and privileges with
themselves. There is as great a difference between real and affected humility as between
practical charity and conventional alms-giving,
or between prayers and confessions in the

spirit, and those which are such only in the letter (Luke 18 : 10–14).

There are many preachers who, in order to reach, as they say, the common people, make themselves really vulgar and mean—pandering to ignorance, prejudice, conceit, superstition, or love of sensation. And on the other hand there are others who stand aloof from the multitude, or if they come in contact with them, touch them only with gloved fingers, preach over their heads, and seek by their social reserve and conventional pietisms to inspire a superstitious awe and veneration for themselves and the church. But neither of these methods is a practical way of applying charity—is not that true humility that exalts, nor that pure unselfishness which beareth all things, hopeth all things, endureth all things. To really show that we love the poor we must take them by the hand, help them to rise and stand on their own feet, and lead them in at the Beautiful Gate. Such contact will not debase us, nor the poor, but will glorify us and them. With this motive the Christ did not hesitate to touch even lepers, or permit a woman who was a sinner to wash his feet; and Paul, when bitten by a viper, shook it off and received no harm. In fact charity's sole purpose is to help the poor to

rise, heal all their infirmities, bring them up to
its own social level, and lead them in with itself at the heavenly Gate. This is the very
best that man or God can do—to give any and
every person the opportunity and means of
helping himself to the utmost of his abilities
and desires,—and this is the end of the law for
righteousness. It removed, so far as this beggar was concerned, all necessity of beggary,
thereby delivering him from the bondage of the
law into the glorious liberty of the sons of God.
Nor is it possible for us to fulfill the law in love
in any other way; for otherwise—if we attempt
to fulfill the law in love by alms-giving only—
we but return to the weak and beggarly elements of the world and our righteousness does
not exceed that of the Scribes and Pharisees.

Doubtless there are now, as there were in the
times of the apostles, a great many beggars and
other social parasites, who may be immediately
redeemed by taking them by the hand and lift-
ing them up in the name and power of Jesus
Christ of Nazareth. That is, there are many
that will respond to such charity with faith,
hope, and personal effort to help themselves, receive strength to stand upon their feet, walk
and leap, and enter in at the gate of the church,
wherein is social redemption; but most prefer

silver and gold, and are unwilling to put forth
proper efforts to work out their own salvation,
and can only be brought to redemption through
the disciplinary processes of the law. Hence
Christian men and women must go out into the
world—into the highways and hedges—and
compel them to come in (Luke 14: 23). And
doubtless as citizens of a common country we
can, through the impartiality and unselfishness
of our Christian character, exert a far greater
influence than others in the reformation and enforcement of the civil laws, whereby social
burdens and privileges may be equalized, and
all individuals and classes be persuaded or compelled to pay their just debts, and discharge
their just duties to society. Indeed, the chief
cause of the present inefficiency of the church
in the practical application of charity to the solution of social problems—to the prevention and
elimination of beggary, dissipation and crime,
and the equitable distribution of wealth—is its
indisposition to enter in and impart the leaven
of the gospel to our political institutions—to
the legislative, judicial, and executive depart-
ments. The chief leaven of the whole body
politic is now selfishness, whereas that of the
true church is charity; and manifestly, if any
individual professing to be Christian and striv-

ing to fulfill the mission of the Christ in the world, does not to the degree of his possible influence impart thereto the leaven of unselfishness, his profession is vain and hypocritical; he becomes a traitor to his trust, and betrays his Master—a blind watchman, blinded through his own selfishness to social inequities and oppressions, a dumb dog that cannot bark at political thieves and robbers through its own greed and dishonesty (Isa. 56: 9–11). Nor can it be denied that our legislative halls abound with such men—lawmakers who profess to be Christians, and are often very zealous workers in the churches, but who are merely political partisans, demagogues, tricksters, jingoes, and pedants, and seemingly totally lacking in real statesmanship or in the spirit of the gospel of peace and brotherhood.

But it must not be forgotten that the proper application of charity to the redemption of the world is very different in its methods from its application to the regulation of our social relations with each other in the church; although it is in either case the expression of the same unselfish love—else it would degenerate into a morbid and inefficient pity, or piety, that condones and excuses offences, and encourages more than it represses sin and selfishness. The true spirit of the law is love, and its enforcement is a work of love; and if we fail to enforce it, when moral suasion fails, we are lacking in love. The Christ did not come to destroy the law; but if we fail to enforce it, we destroy it, and our charity, like the law, is also dead. As a wise father—and no father is wise who is not also loving—chasteneth his disobedient children, so our heavenly Father chasteneth us, and to this end has established the law (Deut. 8: 5, 6; Heb. 12: 5-10; Rev. 3: 19). Applied to the church, love is the practical realization of Fatherhood in God and Brotherhood in Man. Applied to the world, it is the culture through faith and hope of promises not yet realized, and the enforcement of the moral law.

While, therefore, in the true church, in which all members are disposed to do what is right, in conscience sensitive to dishonor, we should bear with each other's infirmities, neither resisting evil nor returning evil for evil—our effort being to fulfill the law in love, and not by compulsion, not requiring an eye for an eye or a tooth for a tooth, but returning good for evil,—yet in the world, so far as men are indisposed to fulfill the law in love, and evil cannot be overcome with good, it is our duty to enforce the law; and if we fail to enforce it, we are un-

merciful and unjust. That is, the same spirit
of non-resistance in the church is the spirit of
resistance in the world—even as the love of
God becomes a consuming fire of righteous in-
dignation and wrath to all persistent and unre-
pentant transgressors of his laws (Deut. 4: 24;
Heb. 12: 29). While it is the imperative duty
of the Christian to forgive all repentant transgressors, and also to give space for repentance,
he but condones and encourages transgressions
if he forgives those who will not repent.
Hence, when we pray, as the Christ prayed,
that God may forgive our enemies, we properly
mean that they may be brought to repentance;
for otherwise we should ask God to condone
their offences—as if he were capricious, and
himself tolerant of evil. No more striking illustrations of the wrath of God are presented in
the Bible than in the example of the Christ in
the awful anathemas he pronounced upon all
men wilfully blinded through selfishness to
their own uncharitableness and personal meanness of character (Matt. 13: 41, 42; 18: 6, 7;
25: 41; Luke 6: 24–26; 10: 13–15; 16: 23, 24).
When in the temple he found those who sold
oxen, sheep, and doves, and the changers of
money, he made a scourge of small cords, and
drove out the oxen and sheep, poured out the

money of the money-changers, and overthrew
their tables, and said unto those who sold
doves, "Take these things hence" (John 2:
14–16).

No Christian man, under the law,—and all
are under the law as Jesus was in his earthly
ministry—will voluntarily submit to evil, but
will, as in duty bound to do, resist it in defence
of the rights and liberties of men, will freely
use the scourge for the repression of every form
of unrighteousness, else he would not be a
moral man and a good citizen of the State—
howbeit he will willingly submit, as his Master
did, to any sacrifice, even of life itself, needful
to the promotion of the well-being of his fellow-
men. Thus Jesus, though he could have called
to his defence more than twelve legions of angels (Matt. 26: 53, 54), yet that the scriptures
might be fulfilled concerning him—that is, that
he might fulfill his mission of unselfish sacrifice—suffered himself to be despised and rejected of men, a man of sorrows and acquainted
with grief, to be wounded for our transgressions, and made to bear our iniquities, not
opening his mouth, but suffering himself to be
led as a lamb to the slaughter—thus voluntarily
undergoing this needful sacrifice in his conflicts
with sinful men. He could also have armed

his followers with carnal weapons and have resisted the officers of the law, yet forbade Peter
to use the sword (John 18: 10, 11); for otherwise—had he not drunk the cup his Father had
given him to drink, not been tempted in all
things as we are tempted, not been formed in
fashion as a man, not humbled as we are humbled, nor obedient unto death as we finite, imperfect, and sinful mortals must necessarily be
—he could not have been an example we could
follow.   That is, more would have been required of us than he himself was willing to endure, and he would have avoided the trials we
in our weakness are compelled to endure.   He
did not come into the world to teach us what
he could do for himself, but what we can do for
ourselves in enduring and overcoming evil, and
in securing the favor and help of God through
faith, hope, and charity.   He could through his
superior knowledge and power have escaped the
persecutions of his enemies, and all other evils
incident to this earthly life, but he could not
have fulfilled his mission otherwise than by
voluntarily suffering what we are compelled to
suffer through our sinfulness and consequent
weakness, and what cannot be removed except
through the discipline of the law, and our voluntary fulfillment thereof in love.

Having therefore, put himself precisely in our place, the Christ did not use superhuman force to defend himself, but used carnal weapons to enforce the law to the extent we can use them to defend ourselves and others by the enforcement of just laws, and so far as they can be made available to promote the well-being of society. And they can be made available so far as our motive is true charity ; that is, so far as love inspires hatred of oppression, and en- kindles wrath against all injustice, selfishness, and sin, but no farther. As a rule, those who take the sword perish with the sword (Matt. 26: 52);—that is, those who rely upon the sword to promote and progagate the principles of the gospel of the Christ—to establish true liberty, equality, and fraternity—will sacrifice their lives in vain, such liberty, equality, and fraternity being only possible of attainment in the practice of mutual reconciliation and love— though the sword may and should be used in defence of the gospel, and in the enforcement of just laws, when the sword that proceedeth out of the mouth fails. Hence, when Jesus was arrested, and his disciples inquired "Lord shall we smite with the sword?" he replied, "Suffer ye thus far" (Luke 22: 49–51), " The cup which my Father hath given me shall I not drink?" (John 18: 11); yet only a moment before he had said, "He that hath no sword, let him sell his garment and buy one" (Luke 22: 36; Rom. 13: 4).

While, therefore, in teaching us what we can do, he did not often use carnal weapons,—never, in fact, in the promulgation of his gospel (2 Cor. 10: 3-6)—yet we greatly err if we suppose charity to be wholly peaceful, and cry, "Peace, peace, when there is no peace" (Jer. 6: 14; Matt. 10: 34), for such charity, like faith without works, would be dead—cowardly, selfish, and shiftless; or that when he counseled his disciples not to resist evil he enunciated a principle applicable to a sinful world, and practicable in a society necessarily subject to the bondage of the law, which by command of God requires an eye for an eye and a tooth for a tooth. Thus to condemn mob violence, and yet do nothing to right the wrongs of our fellow-men enslaved to the mammon of unrighteousness, is to cry, Peace, peace, when there is no peace, and renders us partakers in the guilt and cruelty of the oppressor. What God is in the Church such also is he in the world, without variableness or shadow of turning—always loving, merciful, and just—and this invariableness requires that he should deal differently with men in their different relations to him. When men, though still imperfect, are believers in his gospel of peace and mutual reconciliation, and are striving to dwell together in accordance with such principles, he counsels them not to resist evil, but to overcome evil with good—that when one smites us on the cheek we should turn the other also; for by such example any person who is striving to live in obedience to the gospel will be led to repent, and seek forgiveness from us for the injury he has done. But in the world, when men are indifferent to the gospel, or enemies thereof, he requires all men who wilfully and persistently transgress his laws to be punished. Surely, the Christ does not require us to do differently from what his Father in Heaven would do.

Indeed it would be extreme cruelty to require us to submit unnecessarily to any injustice—although we should be willing to endure any sacrifice needful for the promotion of the well-being of men. Thus it is an error to suppose God sent his Son into the world with the intent that he should be put to death, for his sole purpose was that the world through him might be saved—howbeit, because of the wickedness of the world, he knew that Jesus would be put

to death. So also he sends us into the world
to preach and teach by our example the principles of the gospel, and to endure all persecutions and sacrifices requisite to the fulfillment
of our mission. But he does not require us to
endure evil needlessly—to cast pearls to swine
which trample them in the mire, and then turn
and rend us (Prov. 9: 7-9; Matt. 7: 6; Acts
13: 45, 46). Indeed the Christ expressly requires us to withdraw our peace from those
who will not receive us, and to shake off their
dust from our feet, for it will be more tolerable
for the people of Sodom and Gomorrah in the
day of judgment than for them (Matt. 10:
13-15; Acts 13: 51). Withdrawing our peace
from any man is leaving him to be dealt with
according to the law; and as we are citizens of
the State, and under the law, we must deal
with him as the law requires. Even a member
of the church when excommunicated, is delivered to the discipline of the law (Matt. 18:
17). So also all persons who deal unjustly
(Matt. 18: 23-35). Hence, so far from teaching that his gospel is wholly peaceful, the
Christ requires us to resist and punish evil
doers who cannot be brought to repentance by
the preaching of the gospel (Matt. 22: 2-15).

While, therefore, in the church we may have

peace, in the world we must have tribulations (John 16: 33). While in the church we may be free from any obligations of duty, debt, or sacrifice, yet in the world we are subject to all obligations the law imposes upon us ; and if we seek to avoid such obligations by pleading our Christian principle of non-resistance to evil, or that, being Christians, we have no right to meddle with politics, we cease to be Christians; for our mission, like that of the Christ, is to the world. To pay taxes to Cæsar and to render unto him the things that are his, is to make, obey, and enforce just laws. In this way only—by becoming Christians, and at the same time discharging our debts to the world—can we render unto Cæsar the things that are Cæsar's and unto God the things that are God's, and overcome the world (John 16: 33). The church on earth is militant, all true members being soldiers of Christ, taking to themselves " the whole armor of God," which necessarily includes the moral law, that they may " wrestle against principalities, against powers, against the rulers of the darkness of this world, against spiritual wickedness in high places "— though we wrestle not with flesh and blood, as does " the warrior with confused noise, and garments rolled with blood," but " with burn-

ing and fuel of fire" (Isa. 9: 5),—with impas-
sioned love of righteousness, and the burning
and fuel of wrath and hatred against all injustice and oppression. While the sword of
the gospel is a spiritual weapon, and proceedeth
out of the mouth (Rev. 1: 16), that of the law
is carnal, and used for discipline, punishment,
and compulsion (1 Chron. 21: 16 ; Rom. 13: 4).

True charity, therefore, applied to the world,
is that which is sustained by a stern sense of
justice, an unfaltering moral courage to do and to
dare whatever God requires, and while it loves
God with all its heart, soul, and mind, and its
neighbor as itself, beareth, believeth, hopeth,
endureth all things, and is kind, it yet hates all
injustice, cruelty, and oppression with equal in-
tensity, passion, and persistency. Being in
fact the impersonation, word, and expression of
God who is Love Itself, it like him uses the
sword of the Spirit that proceedeth out of the
mouth, but when that fails to bring men to repentance, it uses also the sword of resistance,
discipline, and punishment.

Now if men are not in the Church they are
under the law, or otherwise at the mercy of the
mob, which has no sense of mercy or justice.
And, since as has been shown, it is impossible
to be free under the law—it having been es-

tablished because of our offences, whereby it became necessary to place us under duress—it is plain that through the charity of the gospel only, whereby men are led to willing obedience to God, can they become free from the bond-age of the law. Yet the bondage of the law may be lightened to the degree the law is leavened with the spirit of the gospel; and to the degree the Christian is under the law, so may the men of the world be brought under the influence of the gospel, and in time both the law and the gospel become one in God (1 Cor. 15: 28). Hence, for the promotion of our own freedom in the world, as well as that of others, must we strive so to apply our charity to the world as will promote liberty, equality, and fraternity. The Christian life is a warfare, a struggle for liberation and escape from the cruel bondage of social and political oppression —from the Pharaohs of the world—and is a journey through the wilderness, wherein are fiery serpents and scorpions and drought (Deut. 8: 15), in which great and mighty kingdoms of this world are to be subdued or blotted out. And so long as there are inequities in the world must this conflict be continued, and perfect freedom and peace be impossible of realization.

And finally, it being manifestly true, that

practically to apply our Christian charity to the
world, we must strive to give every man an
equal chance with his fellow-men for improvement in his social conditions and relations—of
increase in health, knowledge, wealth, happiness, and power,—we must, in accordance with
the letter and spirit of the natural and moral
laws of God, endeavor to the utmost of our
power to persuade, and so far as is necessary to
compel, all men to obey such laws. And to
this end we must so modify, improve, and enforce our civil laws—abolishing some and en-
acting others—as will secure equal opportunities of social redemption to all citizens ; for, as
previously shown, it would be vain and hypocritical to attempt to inspire Christian hope
without at the same time striving to give the
poor and oppressed the means and opportunity
of realizing such hope. In fact, it is otherwise
impossible practically to possess and apply charity, which is the fruitage of hope. But it is of
course impossible, within the limits of this
work, to define very much in detail what true
charity requires in the way of legislation.
The gospel sets before us the mark to which
we should press forward, forgetting the things
which are past—the mark being the true ideal
of social life in the Church of Christ—yet at

the same time requires us to work out our own salvation in the fear and by the help of God (Phil. 2: 12, 13), meeting and overcoming all difficulties in our path as they arise. We can, however, on the authority of the law and the gospel, define in a measure, as we have already done in previous parts of this work, what our objective purpose should be, and how the obstacles which now confront us may be overcome.

Doubtless the most serious obstacle which the Christian citizen encounters in his efforts to apply practically the charity of the gospel, is the world's love of money, its devotion to the Golden Calf,—which, even though we hate, we are compelled to worship, to "the world, the flesh and the devil," personified in the Scarlet Woman, by whom all the inhabitants of the earth have been made drunk with the wine of her fornication (Rev. 17). And this idolatry and fornication is equally manifest among rich and poor, the uncrowned millionaire princes and kings of society (12), and its professional beggars, prodigals, and thieves.

Now we need not be led into a lengthy discussion of what money is—except to say that it is primarily intended, as a matter of convenience, to be a medium of exchange, and as such is harmless, but has become in fact an object of idolatry, cupidity and worldliness, and, though intrinsically of little or no value or necessity, has by our corrupted art been made to represent the highest values of life, and become an absolute necessity to our existence—representing in fact an arrogancy of authority superior to that of God; not only assuming power to represent the inalienable rights and possessions he alone can bestow, but also to traffic therein, and to purchase or sell titles thereto according to the caprices, passions, and cupidities of finite and selfish men.

As the love of money is a root of all evil, it is impossible to overcome all evils except this root be exterminated—or indeed any evil; for if otherwise any social evil be temporarily suppressed, from the same root it will be reproduced, and will become an endless succession of evils. Being artificially made the primary interest and necessity, money subjects all other interests to itself, so that society becomes utterly enslaved thereby and thereto. Representing all values, it concentrates all values in itself, and monopolizes all interests and necessities. And having monopolized all interests and necessities, it perpetuates such monopolies by civil laws, so-called, which, though directly in conflict with the spirit of natural and moral laws, are craftily, arrogantly, and hypocritically claimed to represent in themselves the supreme authority of divine law.

But it is of course the love of money, not money itself, that is a root of all evils. The golden calf is harmless if not made an object of worship. Hence, if the love of money be suppressed, money may still be used, as a convenient medium of exchange without detriment to society. Nor is it money that develops the love of money, nor the golden calf that develops the worship thereof, it being a senseless thing incapable of responding to or inspiring love or worship, but the selfishness, cupidity and worldliness of sinful men, who arbitrarily affix fictitious values thereto, and confer upon it unnatural powers, thereby converting its convenience into the opportunity of acquiring exclusive and unrighteous privileges, immunities and impunities.

But while no argument is needed to prove that the gifts of God cannot be purchased with money, or that a golden calf cannot listen to or grant our prayers, it is yet a fact that Satan, the Father of lies (John 8 : 44), otherwise defined as the "Mammon of Unrighteousness," the Demon of Human Avarice personified, can

and does for a time possess all the kingdoms of
the earth, and confer them upon those who fall
down and worship him (Matt. 4: 8, 9).   And
this he does by perverting, through our ignorance or selfish cupidity, our natural and instinctive perceptions of what is just and right,
so that what is unjust and wrong appears to be
right.   Thus it is manifestly just and right that
we should obey the higher powers (Rom. 13: 1–
4)—it being understood that such powers are
ministers of God for our good, all authority being derived from God,—yet if such higher
powers are themselves selfish, they are ministers
for good only in seeming ; are in fact tyrants,
and ministers of evil, although their authority
may seem to be genuine, derived of God, and
even the laws they enact and enforce be just
and righteous in the letter, though administered
in the spirit of selfishness and cupidity.
Doubtless it is right, for example, that the
highest authority in the nation should coin and
issue money so far as the convenience and necessity of the people require in the interchange
of useful commodities, but it has no right to
endow it with unnatural prerogatives and
powers.   To be sure it is a senseless and harmless thing in itself, as is a golden calf, and for
this reason cannot itself be held responsible for

the evils it evolves and develops, but if used, as a knife in the murderer's hand, to rob men of their natural and inalienable rights of life, liberty, and the pursuit of happiness,—to deprive them of the free use of earth, water, air, sunshine, and even of their own personal endowments and faculties of body and mind, which God bestows equally upon all men, even to compel them to neglect and violate all his natural, moral, and spiritual laws, and to forego and repress all natural hopes and aspirations for improvements—it becomes an instrument in the Unrighteous Mammon's hand for the consummation of all villainies and crimes. Indeed no person or government can have any just right to possess or do anything in the spirit of selfishness, however otherwise observant he may be of the letter of the laws of God; for the true spirit of all such laws is mercy, justice, and charity. And while every man has a natural right to do what he will with his own, yet as all are social beings, and no one can live unto himself alone, no individual or class, can rightfully do or possess anything at all, exclusive of or prejudicial to, the rights and best interests of his fellow-men.

As God's gifts cannot be rightfully alienated except by misuse thereof in violation of God's

laws, the Government—which is the agency of
God, and the custodian of his gifts for their
just and equal distribution among the people—
cannot rightfully make them alienable, or permit them to become articles of traffic by esti-
mating their value by a standard of gold or
silver. This, therefore, is the problem we are
to solve. How shall we limit the use of money
to the exchange of such necessities of life as we
by our own industry have lawfully acquired?
Manifestly the first requisite thereto is that the
government withhold from individuals any exclusive or vested titles in fee simple to anything whatever that God has bestowed upon all
men in common—although it may and should
distribute equitably among all the use thereof
during their natural lives. Such titles cannot
be justly or rightfully bought, sold, or given
away, and should by law be abolished, and their
acquirement prohibited forever. Moreover, the
money, which the government has put out for
the use and convenience of the people, rightfully and justly reverts to the government at
the death of each individual possessor thereof.
Nor should any individual be permitted to devise or inherit any earthly thing; for whatever
we leave behind is properly the inheritance of
all men in common, and we have no right while

we live to say who shall possess at our decease what we now only temporarily possess. As we brought nothing into this world, we cannot rightfully inherit or possess anything here, except what God has bestowed upon us or given us the right to acquire. Indeed we have no power or right of ourselves to acquire and possess wealth, except it be given us of God (Deut. 8: 17, 18), and manifestly, when we have no longer any use of that we have acquired—it being impossible to take it with us into the next world—it justly reverts to God, and by him is placed in the custody of the government for its equitable distribution among the people, for whose protection and well-being the Nation is responsible. Nothing could be more unjust, and really absurd, than that the rights and possessions of the living should have been determined and established forever by those who are dead.

Thus, the Nation becoming the perpetual custodian and administrator of all estates, and the people in common the inheritors thereof, there will be little use of money, and every person starting out in life will have equal opportunities with all others of possession and increase in all riches; and moreover, there being no excuse for beggary, dissipation, or thievery, all natural and moral laws may and should be enforced with stern justice, and without variableness or shadow of turning. Nor is such legislation as is requisite to secure to all citizens such equal opportunities at all impracticable; nor need it seriously disturb business or other social interests; for while excessive devotion to business would in a proper measure be repressed, the masses of the people would be stimulated to vastly increased and more useful enterprise. Indeed this one legislative act of justice and charity—the total abolition of traffic in God's gifts, and of all personal and exclusive inheritances, devises, or gifts of anything whatever, of public utility and use, except what comes to us naturally, and by divine appointment, would give immediate relief from social stress, and render all social problems comparatively easy of solution—make very straight and smooth in the desert a highway for our God (Isa. 40: 3). All monopolies, private or corporate—being created and controlled by the State, and their property ultimately reverting thereto —would not only cease to be oppressive, but would become blessings. Nor would these be any difficulties in the proper adjustment of wages, profits or taxation—all persons starting out in life personally poor, but with equal and abundant opportunities of securing a livelihood, and really needing nothing more than the State enables them to secure ; the State requiring nothing in the way of taxation but a small rent or usury of such property as she, as the custodian of the gifts of God, and of estates of persons deceased, holds for the common good of all citizens.

But while such legislation would, if enacted, be entirely practicable, and would vastly, immediately, and perpetually increase the wealth, freedom, culture, and happiness of the community, it will doubtless prove very difficult of realization—so blinded are we by selfishness to our own best interests that for the reason the truth is told us we do not believe it (John 8: 43–45 ; 2 Cor. 4: 4) ; both the church and the world so idolatrous or besotted in worldliness that they are no longer valiant in faith (Jer. 9: 1–6 ; Heb. 11: 32–34), or so drunken of the "golden cup" (Jer. 51: 7), and so brutish (Jer. 51: 17) and cruel that they have become insensible to pity (Matt. 18: 33 ; Jas. 5: 5, 11), and deaf to the cries of oppressed and suffering humanity (Ex. 3: 7 ; Job 34: 28 ; Prov. 21: 13).

Many of the poor, "for anguish of spirit, and for cruel bondage" (Ex. 6: 9), will not listen to their Deliverer (Acts 7: 35) sent from God, who cometh out of Sion (Rom. 11: 26, 38), "the Church in the wilderness," but make them gods to go before them—demagogues, flatterers, and deceivers (Num. 16: 1, 12; Ps. 5: 9; Dan. 11: 22; Matt. 24: 5; 2 John 7), who, "while they promise them liberty," themselves are the servants of corruption (2 Pet. 2: 19). Many are so demoralized by servitude that they have lost all sense of manliness, self-respect, and independence, and have become base parasites, sycophants, and toadies to their oppressors, incapable of enduring hardness as good soldiers of Christ (2 Tim. 2: 3), suffering themselves to be driven in gangs as slaves or convicts to their daily tasks; even making a god of the belly, and when delivered from bondage, longing for the flesh-pots of Egypt (Ex. 16: 3; Num. 11: 5, 6).

So also many of the rich, and of those who deem themselves only fairly well to do, wise in their own conceits (Prov. 28: 11), in whose hearts human sympathies are suppressed by the love of money, the word of God choked through the deceitfulness of their riches, puffed up with the pride of life, and whose eyes and ears are so blinded and dulled by the god of this world that they cannot realize their own misery or the inevitable destruction that awaits them in their selfish and cruel indifference to the sufferings of the poor—will vehemently oppose and denounce as fanatical all really practical efforts to apply the love of God to the redemption of their fellow-men. Nay, even professing Christians—pledged in the sacred sacraments of the Church to renounce the world, the flesh, and the devil, and not to follow or be led by them, yet forgetful of their mission to preach the gospel to the poor, to open every prison door, and let the oppressed go free, and like the sow that is washed, returning to their wallowings in the mire (2 Pet. 2 : 22)—are so drunken in the wine of worldliness (Rev. 17 : 3-6) that they will brand as false and heretical the vital principles of the gospel of charity they have professed to believe, and have promised to practice.

Nevertheless there are very many, and a rapidly increasing number, both in Church and State, who have not bowed the knee to the image of Baal (Rom. 11 : 4), and who with God's help will overcome the world. And God will help them—although in his disciplinary providences, whereby he seeks to bring men to repentance, those he loves are for a time necessarily involved, as was the Christ, in sufferings —in the scourges and plagues he visits upon a

sinful world through the operation of his natural laws in which there is no variableness or
shadow of turning. These scourges and plagues
are ten in number, corresponding with the Ten
Commandments of the moral law—all classes
of evils being summarized therein—and also
symbolized in the ten horns of the beast the
Scarlet Woman rode (Rev. 17: 12, 16), and in
the ten plagues visited upon the Egyptians
(Ex. 9: 14). And how plainly manifest, and
yet how blinded our eyes thereto by the god of
this world, that God is now visiting upon us the
same scourges and plagues he visited upon the
Egyptians for our cruel social oppressions,
whereby the poor and distressed are compelled
to make bricks without straw, and even to bar-
ter virtue for bread. Moreover, it is especially
to be noted that, as Haman perished upon the
gallows he himself erected, so a wicked world,
through its own selfish greed, is made to create
the deadly scourges and plagues with which it
is afflicted, in accordance with the universal and
just laws whereby with what measure we mete
it is measured to us again (Matt. 7: 2), and we
are compelled to reap what we sow (Gal. 6:
7, 8). Thus through greed of money, whereby
every consideration of health is recklessly sacrificed to what is called business interests, our

naturally pure fountains and streams are converted into filthy and bloody waters, whereby the fish that swim therein, and the animals and men that drink thereof, sicken and die; the air we are compelled to breathe befouled, and hordes of vermin generated—lice, flies, and countless other varieties of other moths, rusts, and thieves, to consume, waste, and plunder our fruits and harvests, as also the works of art we weave and construct; tormenting murrains, blains, and malignant and deadly diseases and pestilences evolved and developed of adulterated and poisoned foods and drinks, and the unnatural conditions in which we are compelled to live; frightful and destructive floods, earthquakes, tornadoes, and tempests of fire and hail developed of the just wrath of God—all of which naturally result from our transgressions of natural laws, and are Nature's efforts to purify itself from our pollutions thereof.

But as leprosy and all other diseases otherwise incurable were healed by the touch of Christ's finger, and even the tempests stilled at his command (Matt. 8: 2; Mark 4: 39), so may all curses and plagues with which the human race is afflicted be removed by contact of the true Church with the world. And it can touch the world if we cast out the motes of selfishness and cupidity from our own eyes, whereby we are enabled to see clearly to cast out the motes from the eyes of our brother men. If we purify ourselves from our worldliness, and fulfill our mission to the world, we can purify the world, and heal all its infirmities —bind up all that are bruised, and open every prison door.

Or if the world itself, which Satan hath bound, lo! these centuries of cruel bondage (Luke 13: 16), would but touch in faith the living Church, the hem of Christ's garment. (Mark 5: 27–29; Rom. 8: 21–26), every fountain of tears and blood would be dried, and it would feel in its body that it was healed of every plague. "O earth, earth, earth, hear the word of the Lord" (Jer. 22: 29), and thou shalt know the truth, and the truth shall make thee free (John 8: 32);—break every yoke, burst every bond, and open every iron gate of oppression (John 30: 8; Acts 12: 7, 10). Let all or any brotherhoods, confederations of labor or capital, political parties, or socialistic organizations—most or all of which are now practically oppressive monopolies, each selfishly striving to promote its own exclusive interests by increased prerogatives, immunities, impunities, wages, or profits, regardless of the rights or interests of others,—adopt, and incorporate into their constitutions, declarations of principles, or articles of confederation, the fundamental principles of Divine Law and Love, they will, if true to their avowed principles, become one in spirit and purpose, obtain control of the Government, and secure the just rights and liberties of all citizens; for as the people are, so inevitably will be the Government, so far as they cherish the true principles of religion, and understand how such principles may be applied to the practical realization of liberty, equality, and fraternity. Nor can any person who rightly interprets the signs of the times seriously question that the fullness of time has come for such practical realization of the principles and promises of the gospel of the Christ. We are certainly on the threshold of a new dispensation of the gospel—a great renaissance of natural, moral, and spiritual culture. The Christ in spirit is coming again— his Kingdom nearer at hand than when we believed (Rom. 13: 11, 12). It is high time to awake out of sleep. The night is far spent, the day is at hand. Let us cast off the works of darkness, and put on the armor of light, that we may wrestle against principalities and powers, against spiritual wickedness in high places both in Church and State. The congregations of the Church are opening their eyes to the discernment of the fundamental truths and principles upon which liberty, equality, and fraternity are founded, and our social salvation realized—casting away sectarian dogmas and ordinances of man's appointment, whereby we are prevented from becoming One in the Brotherhood of Christ, and sore hindered in running the race set before us; they are rising above old superstitions, bigotries, and gross literalisms in interpretations of the word of God, whereby we have been made blind and dead to the spirit thereof (John 6: 63; 8: 46, 47; 1 Cor. 2: 14; 2 Cor. 3: 6). The skies of our religious, social, and political lives are wondrously brightening. Wise men, hitherto blinded by our superstitions to the light shining in darkness, and standing aloof from the Church, are now again following the guidance of its bright and morning Star (Matt. 2: 2; Rev. 22: 16). The New Jerusalem, the golden city of peace and brotherhood, the living Church of the living God (1 Tim. 3: 15; Rev. 21: 10), is visibly descending from heaven. "And I heard a great voice out of heaven, saying, Behold the tabernacle of God is with men, and he shall dwell with them, and they shall be his people, and God himself shall be with them, and be their God. And God shall wipe away all tears from their eyes ; and there shall be no more death, neither sorrow nor crying. Neither shall there be any more pain, for the former things have passed away." And the Spirit of Truth, and of the true and living Church (1 John 16: 13; Eph. 5: 33; Rev. 21: 2, 9), say, Come. And let him that heareth the voices thereof (Ezek. 43: 2; Matt. 11: 28; John 18: 37) say, Come. And let him who is athirst for a purer fountain of life, or ahungered for a larger liberty and a nobler manhood (Isa. 55: 1, 2; John 4: 14; 6: 27, 35, 58; 8: 36), say, Come. And let all who would love God and their brother men, and be loved of them (Matt. 22: 37-40: 1 Cor. 2: 9; 1 John 4: 20, 21), say, Come—enter in at the Beautiful Gate, " walking, leaping, and praising God."

www.ingramcontent.com/pod-product-compliance
Lightning Source LLC
Chambersburg PA
CBHW021108270326
41929CB00009B/776